CATCH
Program Guide

Catch: A Churchwide Program for Invitational Evangelism

Program Guide with DVD ROM

Everything needed for the pastor or leadership team to plan the program

978-1-42267-4347-4

Small Group Participant Book

Four-week adult study to get the congregation on board

978-1-4267-4301-6

Small Group DVD with Leader Guide

Inspirational videos for four small group sessions

978-1-4267-4161-6

Implementation Guide

Follow up guide for leadership group or implementation team

978-1-4267-4300-9

Catch Kit

One of each component

843504028459

CATCH

A CHURCHWIDE PROGRAM FOR
INVITATIONAL EVANGELISM

Program Guide

Debi Nixon
with Adam Hamilton

Abingdon Press / Nashville

Special thanks to Jenny Youngman, series editor for the Catch *program.*

CATCH: PROGRAM GUIDE
DEBI NIXON WITH ADAM HAMILTON
COPYRIGHT © 2012 BY ABINGDON PRESS
ALL RIGHTS RESERVED.

Except as noted, no part of this work may be reproduced or transmitted in any form or by any means, electronic or mechanical, including photocopying and recording, or by any information storage or retrieval system, except as may be expressly permitted by the 1976 Copyright Act or in writing from the publisher. Requests for permission should be addressed in writing to Abingdon Press, 201 Eighth Avenue South, P.O. Box 801, Nashville, TN 37202-0801 or e-mailed to permissions@abingdonpress.com.

Scripture quotations, unless otherwise indicated, are from the Common English Bible, Copyright © 2010 by Common English Bible. All rights reserved. Used by permission. www.CommonEnglish.Bible.com.

Scripture quotations marked (NIV) are taken from the Holy Bible, New International Version®, NIV®. Copyright © 1973, 1978, 1984, 2011 by Biblica, Inc.™ Used by permission of Zondervan. All rights reserved worldwide. www.zondervan.com. The "NIV" and "New International Version" are trademarks registered in the United States Patent and Trademark Office by Biblica, Inc.™

Scripture quotations marked NRSV are from the New Revised Standard Version of the Bible, copyright 1989, Division of Christian Education of the National Council of the Churches of Christ in the United States of America. Used by permission. All rights reserved.

Scripture quotations from THE MESSAGE. Copyright © by Eugene H. Peterson 1993, 1994, 1995, 1996, 2000, 2001, 2002. Used by permission of NavPress Publishing Group.

Scripture quotations marked TNIV are taken from the Holy Bible, Today's New International Version®. Copyright © 2001, 2005 Biblica, Inc.™ All rights reserved worldwide. Used by permission of Biblica, Inc.

This book is printed on acid-free, elemental chlorine-free paper.

ISBN 978-1-4267-4347-4

12 13 14 15 16 17 18 19 20 21—10 9 8 7 6 5 4 3 2

MANUFACTURED IN THE UNITED STATES OF AMERICA

Contents

Foreword by Adam Hamilton 7

Welcome to *Catch* 11

The Program 15

1. Becoming Relentlessly Outward Focused 19

2. Answering Three Important Questions 29

   Check Point: Looking Inward

3. Attracting People in Your Community 43

4. Making Visitors Feel Welcome 59

5. Connecting and Following Up With Visitors 75

6. Inviting Others to Grow in Faith 83

   Check Point: Moving Outward

DVD ROM Documents 101

Foreword
by Adam Hamilton

In your local community it is likely that at least 50 percent of the people are not active in a church family. Half of the people, right there in your neighborhood, do not go to church. Often they consider themselves "spiritual but not religious." These are our children and grandchildren, nieces and nephews, neighbors and co-workers. You might wonder: How does God look at these non-religious people? What does God expect our church to do in order to reach out to them?

As you begin to cast your nets wide with this invitational evangelism program, let's first look to Scripture to set the stage for your work. A pivotal Scripture passage for Jesus' ministry and for our churches today is Ezekiel 34. Through the prophet Ezekiel, God spoke to the civic and religious leaders of the Jewish people and said,

> Woe to the shepherds of Israel who only take care of themselves! Should not shepherds take care of the flock? You eat the curds, clothe yourselves with the wool and slaughter the choice animals, but you do not take care of the flock. You have not strengthened the weak or healed the sik or bound up the injured. You have not brought back the strays or searched for the lost. You have ruled them harshly and brutally. So they were scattered because there was no shepherd, and when they were scattered they became food for all the wild animals. My sheep wandered over all the mountains and on every high hill. They were scattered over the whole earth, and no one searched or looked for them. I myself will search for my sheep and look after them. As a shepherd looks after his scattered flock when he is with them, so will I look after my sheep. I will rescue them from all the places where they were scattered on a day of clouds and darkness. I will bring them out from the nations and gather them from the countries, and I will bring them into their own land. I will pasture them on the mountains of Israel, in the ravines and in all the settlements in the land. I will tend them in a good pasture, and the mountain heights of Israel will be their grazing land. There they will lie down in good grazing land, and there they

will feed in a rich pasture on the mountains of Israel. I myself will tend my sheep and have them lie down, declares the Sovereign Lord. I will search for the lost and bring back the strays. I will bind up the injured and strengthen the weak, but the sleek and the strong I will destroy. I will shepherd the flock with justice. (Ezekiel 34: 2-5, 11-16 NRSV)

I believe it was this passage that Jesus had in mind when he said, "I am the good shepherd" (John 10:11). Matthew noted that when Jesus looked at the multitudes he had compassion on them because they were "like sheep without a shepherd" (Matthew 9:36). Jesus devoted most of his time to ministry with people who were lost sheep. I believe he was revealing his own heart when he spoke of the shepherd who had one hundred sheep, but who left the ninety-nine behind to "go after the [one] lost sheep until he finds it" (Luke 15:4). The text goes on to say that when the shepherd has found the sheep "he is thrilled and places it on his shoulders. When he arrives home, he calls together his friends and neighbors, saying to them, 'Rejoice with me; I have found my lost sheep.' I tell you that in the same way there will be more rejoicing in heaven over one sinner who repents than over ninety-nine righteous people who do not need to repent" (Luke 15:5-7). Notice the prevalence of joy that comes in finding the lost sheep!

Another metaphor Jesus used is that of a fisherman. He saw himself as a man fishing for people. His fishing was "catch and release." Imagine Jesus catching fish from a small pond filled with scum and silt and algae and then releasing them into the deep and fresh waters of the kingdom of God. Jesus' call to his first disciples and still to us today is, "Come, follow me . . . and I'll show you how to fish for people" (Mark 1:16-18).

As I write this, I've been sitting by a pond where a friend of mine has brought his four-and-a-half-year-old grandson, Drake, to fish. They've carefully chosen the right spot to fish (into the wind) and have brought a variety of lures to try. They cast their lines into the water and slowly reel them in. Most of the time they catch nothing, but today the fish are biting. And every ten minutes or so either Drake or his grandpa shouts, "I've got one! I've got one!" Talk about joy! It doesn't get any better than this for a grandfather and his grandson.

The mission of our churches is to continue the mission of Jesus. We are meant to continue the search for lost sheep. We are meant to continue to fish for people. And there is incredible joy in finding lost sheep and in fishing for people.

I got in my car Sunday after church and found that someone had left a note on the seat that read, "Pastor Adam, thank you for leading a church that would change the course of my life over the years. How I dated, how I treat my wife, how I now raise my son—these are all different because I became a Christian here in this church. I am eternally grateful."

I felt joy in reading his note, but the real joy was in the note itself, which expressed the man's gratitude for meeting and following the Good Shepherd and for swimming in God's seas.

As you cast your nets wide and fish for people in your communities, may you "seek out the lost [and] bring back the strays." This program is a guide to fishing for people. But the process of finding strays and fishing for people is not merely about developing a technique; it is about cultivating a love for lost sheep and discovering the joy of fishing for people.

After an hour of fishing, Drake and his grandpa are heading home. They've caught twelve fish. Their hands are a bit smelly and their bodies a bit sweaty—this happens when you're fishing. But as the boy walks to the car, he turns to me and says, "That was awesome!"

As your congregation rediscovers the joy of fishing, and as they begin to see people's lives changed through the ministry of your church, I suspect you'll hear them say, "That was awesome!"

Welcome to *Catch*

Welcome to the *Catch* program for invitational evangelism. Everything in this program is designed to help you lead your church to become outwardly focused—to become fishers of people outside your church building.

Most churches have mastered an inward focus. We know how to plan for our own members. We know how to program, schedule meetings, and keep the church going for the people who already attend. But shifting the culture to reach people outside the walls is the task to which Jesus calls us when he tells us to fish for people. Ultimately, churches are meant not only to disciple believers but to equip them to reach lost people with God's love. You should know from the very first paragraph of this program that making this culture shift will change just about everything you do; but you will be amazed at the excitement created by a church that is passionate about the ministry of reaching people for Jesus Christ.

Invitational Evangelism

As leaders of your congregation, you may already know that there are many different evangelism techniques. There is missional evangelism—where a church goes out into the community and connects with nonchurchgoers on their own turf to meet them where they are, serve them, and draw them to church. There's *attractional* evangelism—where a church designs as many ways as possible to connect with the community, such as postcard mailings, Easter egg hunts, concerts, sports leagues, and other programs which, by meeting community needs, will draw people into the church.

Catch uses elements of both missional and attractional approaches by making sure your congregation and facilities are inviting and welcoming to any persons you want to reach, whether you are serving in the community or holding events at your church. Think about this approach as *invitational* evangelism.

Why do you need elements of both? Because your church can be all about missional evangelism, going out into the community and meeting people where they live, or it can do a great job of attractional evangelism, creating events to draw people in; but if the new people don't feel welcome when they arrive, then they probably won't return for a second time.

Invitational evangelism helps you use the best features of both missional and attractional evangelism; but most importantly, it will give you practical ideas and tools for making sure your church is welcoming when the outsiders and newcomers arrive at your church.

The Leadership Team

In an ideal setting, a pastor and a group of committed, passionate, dedicated people are meeting regularly to pray about and discern God's vision for your congregation. You might want to pray this prayer of vision:

> *Lord, we long to know and do your will. Grant us the vision to see your plans for your church and the courage and boldness to carry them to completion. In Jesus' name we pray. Amen.*

In order to change the culture of the church from one that focuses inward to one that looks outward, you will need to gather people around a table to lead this vision. You will need people who are willing to examine every point of ministry through the lens of an outsider. These people will need to surrender the nice, comfortable feeling they have when they come to church, because they must be the first to give up their back-row seats to a late-coming visitor. Your leadership team members will need to encourage others and keep the vision of welcoming as a priority in your church. When people in their small groups or Sunday school classes become frustrated by change, your leadership team must remind them that your church has chosen to be outwardly focused.

You will want to choose leaders—whether outspoken or soft spoken—in your congregation and those who have a desire and gift for outreach. These persons will need to be able to imagine an outsider's view of your church experience. Ideally, they will love your church but not so much that they think everything is just fine as it is. The leadership team will help you examine the state of your church's outward focus, lead small groups focused on invitational evangelism, and implement the evangelism techniques laid out in the program.

Maybe your leadership team is already in place. Maybe your church council is best suited to the job. Maybe you have an evangelism team that is focused on the outreach and invitational ministries of your church. Whichever group works best for your church, try to choose the team based on commitment to a vision and the ability to express and carry out that vision for the church. Some ideas for organizing your leadership team can be found at the end of this Program Guide and on the DVD ROM in the document "Inviting the Leadership Team."

Once the leadership team is assembled, the *Catch* program will help them dream together so that your church can "cast the net wide" into your community and fish for people. The program is made up of three phases: Examination, Teaching, and the Launch.

Examination

The very first thing you need to do to begin the *Catch* program is to pray. Pray for openness, guidance, humility, honesty, and for your eyes to be opened.

It is hard work to look at your church with the eyes of an outsider. It can be uncomfortable to realize that you may need to stop doing some things, to do some things differently, or to start doing new things. It is also hard work to be an outwardly focused church and stay committed to that vision. It is easier and more comfortable to program a church for its current members, forgetting that many times these programs and ways of doing ministry can actually serve as barriers for reaching outsiders.

So pray. Pray together and on your own. Pray often. Pray that God would sweep into your church and your community and ignite a passion for reaching lost people. Pray that God would give your church the strong arms to throw out the net as wide as you can and then be the kind of church that welcomes and nurtures new believers into the community.

While covering the church in prayer, the next step is for the pastor and leadership team to read the *Catch* Program Guide together and use the worksheets that follow Chapter 2 and Chapter 6. By doing so, you'll examine and determine the state of evangelism efforts in your church currently, and you'll prepare yourselves to lead the church in going out and "catching" people for God. Together you'll explore the state of your inviting, welcoming, and outreach ministries today; determine where change is needed; and then lead toward action so your congregation becomes relentlessly outwardly focused.

Teaching

Once your leadership team has decided to implement the *Catch* program in your church, you'll schedule a season of teaching in the form of a four-week small group program that can be used in regular small group meetings or Sunday school classes. Your goal during this four-week teaching phase will be to get the whole congregation focused on the call to fish for people.

During the four-week teaching phase, we encourage you to consider a four-week sermon series to support and call attention to the *Catch* program. To assist you with this effort, we have included sermon helps and key Scriptures at the end of the Program Guide and on the DVD ROM in "Sermon Helps and Key Scriptures." Our experience shows that *Catch* has the best chance of success when the program is lifted up in worship

Week One will challenge your church to become relentlessly outward focused. The small group session will help members of your congregation search the Scriptures for Jesus' call to fish for people, go into all the world, and seek the lost. They will assess their comfort level in reaching others, learn techniques for sharing their faith, and explore what it means for a church to be welcoming and inviting.

Week Two will focus on answering three important questions: Why do people need Jesus Christ? Why do people need the church? Why do people need your particular church? These three questions will help members think in ways they may not have before about their relationship with Jesus and how they might share it with others.

Week Three is all about practice. Once you get a clear vision of invitational evangelism and commit your church to become relentlessly outward focused, how do you put that vision into practice?

Week Four helps church members discover the part they need to play as the congregation accepts the call to cast the nets wide and invite others to grow in faith. Church members will talk and pray about how their gifts for ministry and experience can be used to welcome the stranger and become a church that is relentlessly outward focused.

The Launch

After the examination phase led by the leadership team and the teaching phase involving the entire congregation through worship and small groups, your church is ready to launch out and cast the net wide. This is where the program goes from conversation to action.

Because members have been focused on invitational evangelism and have assessed how their personal gifts can be used to do the work of welcoming, you will be in good position to transform your church into a welcoming and invitational community. Work groups will deliver gifts to first-time visitors, staff a welcome center, usher with an eye to welcoming visitors, call people who have been away for several weeks in a row, and other important tasks.

Catch is not a Bible study or church program that can be filed on the shelf. It is designed to ignite a passion in your congregation for reaching people in your community and welcoming newcomers as family members into your church. As you launch out to cast your nets, wholly surrendered to the calling God has placed on your church, expect that God will do more than you could ever ask or imagine. How awesome is that?

The Program

As your leadership team digs into this Program Guide, you will discover a step-by-step approach to changing the culture of your church—from looking inward to moving outward.

The Program Guide is made up of six chapters, with videos to accompany each chapter. (See DVD ROM.) The first two chapters help you imagine how your church could become relentlessly outward focused; the final four chapters give you specific techniques to practice invitational evangelism. After both sections you'll find a worksheet to debrief the chapters and videos, and to determine how the *Catch* approach to invitational evangelism might be lived out in your particular setting.

Your job as a church leader is to carry the vision, communicate it to your congregation, and keep pointing people back when they move away from it. In order to change from an inwardly focused church to an outwardly focused church, you will have to take a hard look at your facilities, welcoming ministries, outreach opportunities, follow-up techniques, and discipleship plans. You will have to put everything on the table and ask yourself, "Would someone who has never been to our church before know where to go and what to do?" and "How does this church activity or ministry help us reach lost people?"

The good news is that you will not do this work alone. Real and lasting change comes when church members catch the vision and help you carry it, when they are equipped to lead parts of the program that match their gifts.

How to Use *Catch*

Step 1: Read through this Program Guide and pray about who in your church might be a good choice for the leadership team. Take a cursory look at how you see your congregation—do you think you are more inwardly or outwardly focused? Watch the video segments on the DVD ROM and familiarize yourself with the other files and resources it contains.

Step 2: Create your leadership team. You may already have teams in place such as an administrative council, an evangelism team, or a vision team that might be a good place to start. Set a meeting to engage them in the vision and give them copies of the Program Guide to read along with you. You may make photocopies or print out copies of the Program Guide for this purpose. A PDF file of the Program Guide can be found on the DVD ROM. Set a few meetings to debrief the guide, fill out the worksheets at the end of each section, and watch the videos on the DVD ROM. Set dates for a sermon series and small group study to launch *Catch* and promote it well.

Step 3: Plan the four-week, congregation-wide small group study and optional sermon series to launch the program with the congregation.

Step 4: Determine how the small group study will be led. Will Sunday school classes study together? Will you form new midweek small groups? Who will teach the classes? How many teachers do you need? How can you get the maximum number of people studying invitational evangelism and joining in the call to become outwardly focused? During this step, small groups and Sunday school classes will use the Small Group Participant Book and the Small Group DVD with Leader Guide.

Step 5: While you are planning and studying, read the Implementation Guide to begin thinking through the next steps for implementation. Choose a person or group (if you'd like, it could be the leadership group) to be your implementation team to organize the various task groups that will be needed. For example, you'll read about having appropriate signage and how it helps new people feel welcomed and less nervous about being in an unfamiliar place when they know where to go. Who would you put on that task? How many people would that team require in your situation? Those are the kinds of detail that the Implementation Guide covers, so every time you see a specific technique, think of who might be a point person when you are ready for the implementation phase.

Step 6: Now it's time for your church to become an outwardly focused congregation. Using the Implementation Guide, your implementation team will organize teams and put next steps in motion. This team will map out the various task groups needed and help church members find the place where their gifts are needed, whether it's in greeting visitors, ushering, delivering visitor mugs, or other important tasks.

Cling to the Call

As you pursue a change from being an inwardly focused church to an outwardly focused church, you can be sure that you will face resistance. Some church members enjoy the cozy comfort of the way things are now. They may not want to make any changes, and if they are honest, they may even say they don't want to grow.

Assure them that this is not just another church-growth program. Your goal is not to be the biggest, coolest church in the community and ruin the warm feeling that they love. Your goal is to reach out to the least, the last, and the lost in your community and take every step necessary to show them the depth of love God has for them. We communicate God's love by the way we welcome, serve, and help others grow in faith. Keep this vision before your congregation, and help them fully embrace the call to fish for people.

Blessings as your church goes fishing!

1. Becoming Relentlessly Outward Focused

1.
Becoming Relentlessly Outward Focused

"The Human One came to seek and save the lost."
—Luke 19:10

A young pastor planted a church in the Midwest. His congregation gathered for their first Sunday morning worship service. The place was alive with excitement about what God would do with their little community. That first Sunday, the pastor preached about focusing on people outside of their doors. He proclaimed the mission of their ministry—that they would be a church concerned more about people who were on the outside rather than on the inside. They would seek out the non-religious and lost people in their area and reach out to them. The whole church was on board. They were ready to be an outwardly focused church.

But, the inevitable happened. They quickly decided they liked the nice, cozy feeling of their church and lost their zeal for looking outward. In a leadership team meeting, a church member told the young pastor that he loved the size of their church and hoped they wouldn't get any bigger than that. The pastor looked around the room, saw the nods of agreement, and wondered what happened. Just weeks earlier he had preached the mission of the church to reach people who did not know Jesus Christ—and in just four weeks the church had turned inward.

That is the story of my church, The United Methodist Church of the Resurrection. Because our pastor, Adam Hamilton, clung to the vision of reaching non-religious and nominally religious people in our area, we have grown from that small church to a multi-campus congregation today. That meeting was a turning point for us. We could have decided to continue our coziness instead of sticking by that initial vision of reaching out to lost people who need to know the love of God.

Has this happened in your church as well? Have you discovered how easy it is to become so close to those inside the walls of your church that you lose concern for those outside the walls? But these close relationships can actually serve as a barrier that keeps other people out. When visitors arrive, we're so busy talking and sharing inside stories that the visitors feel like outsiders from the minute they walk in. The worship service itself may communicate that it's only for people who already know what to do and when to do it—not for those who may be attending church for the first time ever.

Very few of us would admit we are this kind of inwardly focused church. We think we are friendly. We'll often defend our friendliness and ignore the fact that visitors cannot find a place in our community. In reality, if we truly examine everything our church does, we might find it is really designed for the benefit of the inside group.

Looking Out

When we decide that evangelism is essential, we take the first step to becoming a church that is relentlessly outward focused. The outwardly focused church looks at everything it does and asks, "How can this help us reach non-religious and nominally religious people?" and "Would a first-time visitor have a sense of what is important here?"

Unfortunately, it is easy for churches to become inwardly focused and more interested in the people inside the walls of the church, neglecting those outside the walls. We begin to focus the church on the things we are interested in, to the exclusion of those outside. It is so easy to forget that there are broken people, strays, and lost sheep outside (and inside) the walls, whom God longs for us to reach. Because of this inclination to focus on ourselves, leaders must constantly remind church members why they exist—for those who do not yet know the love of God.

When I visit with church leaders, I repeatedly hear the comment, "My church is in a dying community," or "My church is in a rural area where everyone is already connected." I have to be honest and tell you what crosses my mind: "Are you really saying there is no one left in your community or surrounding area who doesn't know Jesus Christ?"

Both my parents are from communities with populations of less than two thousand people. I often visit family members living in these areas. When I do, I see small children on the streets riding bicycles. I pass farms. I drive by mobile homes. I see people congregated at the front of the local grocery store. I see an elderly woman sitting alone in her wheelchair in front of the nursing home. When I see these people, I feel the passionate conviction that unless every one of them has a personal, life-transforming relationship with Christ, our work is not done yet. So I ask you: Are there lost people in your community? Even just one?

Jesus came to seek and to save the lost. He left us three parables of lost things: a lost sheep, a lost coin, and a lost son. In each story, just one thing went missing, but Jesus communicates to us the importance of searching until that one lost thing is found. If we take Jesus' teaching seriously, then we as a church have to consider whether we are focused inwardly on the "found" or out fishing for the lost in our community.

Recently, I was in a meeting when a denominational leader responded to the idea that a church is declining because it is in a declining area. With a twinkle in his eye, the leader said, "I guess Jesus Christ is not as strong today as the sociological forces of my community."

Now, that's thought provoking!

Clarity of Purpose

Sometimes the church's biggest hindrance to evangelism is a lack of clarity around its purpose, a poor knowledge of the community and needs of its people, or a poor understanding of what is needed to reach people outside the church. As the leader of your church, you must cast a clear vision of the purpose to which God has called your church, and you must know the needs of your community. That vision will be different for each community and context.

Whatever the setting, Jesus was clear about his purpose. He was resolute in doing what his Father had called him to do. Growing churches are clear on their purpose, and they resolutely set out to work with God to accomplish that purpose.

Having a clear purpose as a church means you know why you exist. At my church, we know why we exist. Our purpose is clearly understood by everyone in our congregation. Our purpose statement defines everything we do: To build a Christian community where non-religious and nominally religious people are becoming deeply committed Christians.

Every person in leadership, and we hope most of our members, can recite this purpose statement from memory. The purpose statement is written in sixteen-inch letters in the narthex of our church so that all who enter or leave our building are reminded of why we exist. Visually, we have four tapestries that hang in our church. Each tapestry illustrates a scene from Jesus' life and ministry: his birth (Luke 2:1-20), his forgiveness of a sinful woman (Luke 7:36-50), his ministry to a tax collector (Luke 19:1-10), and his resurrection (Luke 24:1-9).

The scenes show how Jesus reached out in love, offering forgiveness and salvation to the people whom society had abandoned, ostracized, or ignored—the least, the last, and the lost. The tapestries serve as visual reminders of our purpose to reach out to the non-religious and nominally religious in our community.

Every church meeting has the purpose statement at the top of the agenda. It is in front of us during our planning meetings, in which we design sermon series, worship elements, new programs, brochures and flyers, and fellowship events; and even in business meetings, when we determine finances or make decisions as trustees or the church council, we ask ourselves, "How will this help a non-religious or nominally religious person become a deeply committed Christian?" If we don't have a compelling answer, we don't do that particular program or we will rewrite a brochure to make certain the message is consistent and clear. Our purpose statement guides all that we do. We are relentlessly outward focused.

We learn this from Jesus, who always knew his purpose. Luke 19:10 tells us that "the Human One came to seek and save the lost." He did not focus only on those who had already decided to follow him, but instead demonstrated an outward approach:

> Jesus traveled among all the cities and villages, teaching in their synagogues, announcing the good news of the kingdom, and healing every disease and every sickness. Now when Jesus saw the crowds, he had compassion for them because they were troubled and helpless, like sheep without a shepherd. (Matthew 9:35-36)

If the church is the body of Christ, we must have the same heart as Christ. The heart of Christ was compassion for lost people. Our churches exist to proclaim the good news to lost people. If we take Jesus' teachings seriously, then as a church we have to consider whether we are focused inward on the "found," or are out there fishing for people.

Fishing for People

In order to catch fish, first you must learn how to fish. You have to learn the fishing conditions in the area. You have to check the weather. You have to get the right equipment and master the proper techniques. And you have to go where the fish are!

If followers of Jesus are called to fish for people, we must go where the people are. Sometimes churches forget this simple fact and instead just hang out their OPEN sign, hoping that people will pour in.

Remember the children's rhyme "Here is the church, here is the steeple, open the doors and see all the people"? You probably remember the actions that went with it: holding closed fists, hiding your fingers inside, then opening the "doors" to reveal all the "people." When we reflect on this idea, we might question the theology behind it. Why is the church hidden behind tightly closed fists? Why do you have to open the doors to see the people? Shouldn't the rhyme begin a different way? We could open our hands, wiggle our fingers, and say something like, "Here is the church, see all the people, who have opened the doors to welcome new people."

As the body of Christ, we have a great responsibility to represent God's physical presence in the world—to be outwardly focused, going into the community, casting the net wide, reaching lost people for Christ. We should be churches with open doors, welcoming in new people. But too often, the church that visitors experience is the church represented in this children's rhyme by our tightly interlocked hands. New people arrive and encounter a closed door they have to open, and when they walk inside they see a church full of people who seem to be the church for one another, focused more on their own needs than on the needs of visitors.

We don't intentionally start out to be churches hidden in closed fists; it happens gradually, and many times we don't recognize the type of church we have become. It takes a leader—perhaps someone like you—to remind the church: "No, we are not going that way; this is the way we are going. We will be outwardly focused in all that we do."

Sharing the Heart of God

The church is the body of Christ—the physical incarnation of Jesus in the world—and Scripture provides a model for how we are to be the church. As we read about Jesus' ministry here on earth, we discover the heart of Jesus. We see what motivated and inspired him.

Read how the Book of Ezekiel compares the heart of God to the heart of a shepherd:

> The LORD's word came to me: Human one, prophesy against Israel's shepherds. Prophesy and say to them, The LORD God proclaims to the shepherds: Doom to Israel's shepherds who tended themselves! Shouldn't shepherds tend the flock? You drink the milk, you wear the wool, and you slaughter the fat animals, but you don't tend the flock. You don't strengthen the weak, heal the sick, bind up the injured, bring back the strays, or seek out the lost; but instead you use force to rule them with injustice. Without a shepherd, my flock was scattered; and when it was scattered, it became food for all the wild animals. My flock strayed on all the mountains and on every high hill throughout all the earth. My flock was scattered, and there was no one to look for them or find them. (Ezekiel 34:1-6)

Ezekiel was writing during the Jewish exile in Babylon, and the Jewish people wondered why God had let the Babylonians conquer them. Their Temple had been destroyed, their capital city had been ruined, and they had been carried away as slaves. Ezekiel tells them why in this chapter: it was because the leaders of Israel, the shepherds of God's people, failed to do the things that God expected of them. Instead, they focused on their own needs. Look again at the Scripture text. God says, "You don't strengthen the weak, heal the sick, bind up the injured, bring back the strays, or seek out the lost."

The heart of God is that we care for the weak, sick, and injured; bring back those who have strayed; and search for those who are lost. As pastors and church leaders, we are the shepherds of God's flock. We are the shepherds of the church. Even though you may be an inwardly focused church now, you can make a change. You can begin to focus on reaching the lost people in your community and on caring for the weak, sick, and injured. When you make a decision to change, your church members might become a little uncomfortable. Your new focus might require new resources or new priorities. But don't despair. Keep on pointing to the heart of God and the ministry of Jesus. Take direction from Jesus' life and words about fishing for people.

Relentlessly Outward Focused

Here are two pictures of what churches can look like:

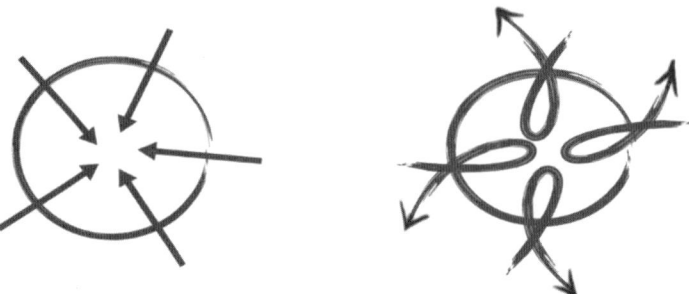

In the first picture, we have a church that is inwardly focused. It is a close church family where those on the inside are building up and supporting one another, but the relationships actually serve as a barrier to keep other people out. Everything they do is focused inward. If I arrive as a visitor, everybody is so close to one another, talking and sharing inside stories, that I feel like an outsider from the moment I walk in. Almost everything they do is designed for their group. Their focus is solely on what the church can do for those on the "inside." The primary question inwardly focused church members ask is, "What is the church doing for me?"

In the second picture, we have a church that is outwardly focused. Members gather together inside the walls of the church for worship, to be inspired and equipped to go back out and serve in the world. In this church, if I show up as a visitor I am welcomed by a friendly greeter or usher who has been trained to be on the lookout for new people to welcome. The worship service, the printed materials, and the hospitality help me feel welcomed and a part of the group from the moment I walk in. The primary question that outwardly focused churches ask is: "What can the church do to reach more people for Christ and prepare me to go back out into the world to serve?" Every church will naturally tend to be inwardly rather than outwardly focused, but growing churches know the difference and choose the latter.

Jesus was a good shepherd. He found those who were lost and had strayed, he bound up those who were injured, and he calls us to do the same.

> Jesus traveled among all the cities and villages, teaching in their synagogues, announcing the good news of the kingdom, and healing every disease and every sickness. Now when Jesus saw the crowds, he had compassion for them because they were troubled and helpless, like sheep without a shepherd. Then he said to his disciples, "The size of the harvest is bigger than you can imagine, but there are few workers. Therefore, plead with the Lord of the harvest to send out workers for his harvest." (Matthew 9:35-38)

The harvest is plentiful in your community. There are lost people, but too few churches go out into the harvest field. Jesus is pleading for us as his field workers to go out. Jesus went through all the towns and villages. He didn't stay in one place and wait for people to come to him. He went to where the people were. He preached the good news of the Kingdom and healed every disease and sickness. Note especially the verse where Jesus feels compassion when he sees the crowds because they were harassed and helpless, like sheep without a shepherd. Do you see the connection between this verse in Matthew and Ezekiel 34:1-6? I wonder, do you and your church feel the same sense of deep compassion for the broken and those without a church in your community as Jesus felt for those whom he encountered? Are you willing to go out into your harvest field, attracting and connecting with lost people, inviting them to discover a personal, healing, and saving relationship with Jesus Christ as they connect with a community of faith?

What kind of church will you be? One that is inwardly focused, or one that is constantly sending out workers to cast the net wide and bring in those who have yet to experience a personal, life-changing relationship with Jesus Christ?

The fact that you are reading this right now suggests that you want to become an outwardly focused congregation. You want non-religious and nominally religious people to find a home in your church. You want to have a church full of members who are more focused on bringing people in than on getting their favorite pew or parking spot each week.

An aimless expedition without the proper gear will lead to frustration and burnout, and it will probably bear no fruit from the effort. By contrast, a successful outing will involve an intentional effort to chart a course, to study surroundings and conditions, to choose the right "bait," and to learn what to do when you actually bring in a catch!

Take the challenge to become relentlessly outward focused. Hold fast to the vision and carry it out in front of your congregation. Take seriously Jesus' call to fish for people, and as you do, you may just find that you need a bigger net!

To Think About

In this chapter, you thought about ways your church could become relentlessly outward focused. You were challenged to

- look outward
- gain clarity of purpose
- fish for people
- share the heart of God

What are some ways your leadership group can begin moving forward on each of these goals? What are some ways you personally can move forward?

2. Answering Three Important Questions

2.
Answering Three Important Questions

"I must preach the good news of God's kingdom in other cities too, for this is why I was sent."
—Luke 4:43

One summer I watched my teenage daughter and a few of her friends set out to catch fish from the dock of our lake house. They gathered a few fishing poles, loaded into the paddleboat, and headed out about thirty-five feet from the dock. After an hour of casting and reeling in nothing, they returned frustrated and discouraged, declaring that fishing was a "waste of time and boring." When I asked what kind of bait they were using, they responded that they didn't have any bait. They thought the fish would just bite on the hook. I probed further and asked what kind of fish they had hoped to catch. The response was one of puzzlement: "What do you mean, 'What kind of fish?' Fish, of course." They had simply set out to catch "fish" without clarity of purpose, knowledge of the environment, or understanding of what might be needed to actually catch fish.

Understanding why we do the things we do is critically important to living out our purpose. When our church began, we established a clear purpose—to reach non-religious and nominally religious people—and realized we had some work to do. We were going to start calling people to invite them to our worship services, but first we needed to answer three important questions, the answers to which would drive everything else we did and help us live out our purpose statement. You should try to answer the same three questions.

Why do people need Jesus Christ?
Why do people need the church?
Why do people need your particular church?

Why Do People Need Jesus Christ?

The question is not: Why would a relationship with Jesus Christ be a nice thing for people to have in their lives? Rather, the question is, Why do people need Jesus Christ? You are making disciples of Jesus Christ and inviting people to follow him. You are inviting them to change their lives and commit or surrender to Jesus Christ. So why do people need Jesus Christ?

In *Leading Beyond the Walls* (Abingdon Press, 2002), Adam Hamilton writes,

> Jesus Christ is the solution to the deepest longings of the human heart. He is the answer to the most serious problems that plague our society. When Jesus is Lord and the Holy Spirit enters the heart of the believer, we find the empty places filled, and the dark sides of our soul transformed. We are in the process of becoming "new creatures in Christ."... Why do people need Christ? Because without him we will always be lost and our lives will never realize their God-given potential. He opens the door to a whole new world for us. He enriches every life he touches. He changes the world one person at a time, as his kingdom expands the globe. (22-23)

We must be able to communicate the answer to this question to people who are unconvinced of their need for Jesus Christ. We must be able to communicate in a way that is compelling to them, not just to us. But first, we must believe it. It must be something we personally believe so strongly that when we share our conviction with people, they can see it in our eyes and hear it in our tone of voice. We must fundamentally believe that Jesus Christ is essential for being fully human. He is the answer to the deepest longings of our soul.

Why Do People Need the Church?

It's important to remember that you are not only inviting people to follow Jesus, but to become a part of the church. There are those who believe in Jesus Christ but do not believe they need a church. Some are distrustful of organized religion. Some believe the church is narrow-minded and comprised of hypocrites, that all we want is their money. Others feel that the church is irrelevant, out of touch, and boring. So, if these people are not convinced they need organized religion, how do you persuade them that they need the church?

The New Testament makes it clear that the church is not our idea. The church was Jesus' idea. He organized his followers and said, "On this rock I will build my church, and the gates of Hades will not prevail against it" (Matthew 16:18 NRSV). Church leaders must have a fundamental conviction about the absolute necessity of the church if they are going to lead the church. In fact, some research studies in the United States have measured the effect on physical health of being part of a church community. These studies demonstrate that people live longer and are healthier in old age when they have a church family than those who don't have a church family.

I am convinced that we can never be the kind of Christians God wants us to be without other Christians. We need each other. God gave each of us different spiritual gifts. I need your spiritual gifts, and you need mine. I need you to hold me accountable for growing in Christ, and you need me to hold you accountable. I need to pray for you, and I need you to pray for me. When I am sick and in the hospital I need you to come visit me, and when you are sick and in the hospital you need me to come visit you. As a church body, we are able to support one another even in our darkest times. Through community, we have the opportunity to serve others. As a church, we pray for and care for one another.

Right after our family had joined the church, my husband Reed was still trying to be a weekend flag-football warrior and suffered a full Achilles tendon tear while playing at an out-of-state tournament. We returned to Kansas City, where he was sent to the hospital for immediate surgery. When we arrived at the hospital, a small group of people from the church, whom we had only barely met, was waiting to pray for us before Reed went into surgery. They sat with me then and continued to visit during his hospital stay. They brought meals for the next month and helped as I cared for our two toddlers and for Reed. To this day I have never forgotten the blessing of having people I didn't know demonstrate to me tangibly the power and love of a church community.

As a church body, we are able to support one another in our darkest times. When one of our members lost his job, his small group was there to support and encourage him. When the wife of one of our members was killed in a tragic accident, the ministry team where she had volunteered surrounded her family with love and care. When a woman confessed that she was addicted to sleeping pills, it was her pastor who got her the help she needed, while the support groups at church helped her stay accountable and drug free. One of our pastors received a call to go to the ICU, where a man had been told his wife would not survive. When the pastor arrived, the couple's small group was already in the room surrounding him with love and support. As his fellow believers, they were there carrying him through the darkest time in his life. This is what it means to be the church.

We also need the church because we were made to worship God together. In the midst of worship, singing, and praying with other Christians, we experience the presence of the Holy Spirit. We need the church because it provides others with whom we can study Scripture in small group settings and serve alongside in the community. Jesus said that where a few people are gathered, he is there (Matthew 18:20). I experience Christ just by being surrounded by his church gathered in worship, in study, and in serving. Together we are part of something so much bigger than any one of us alone. Together we can accomplish more for God than any of us can do by ourselves.

Why Do People Need Your Particular Church?

When our church was founded, there were dozens of other churches starting at about the same time. So why start another church? What could we offer that might reach someone in a way that other churches might not? We needed to understand clearly what was special about our particular congregation—not what made it better than others, but what made it unique. What would we be known for?

We determined that our church would be about reaching "thinking people" in our community by preaching sermons that spoke to both the heart and the mind. We would offer great programs for children and youth, and we would equip our people to be salt and light in our community through service and outreach. We were also committed to excellence and employed a "whatever it takes" approach to ministry.

During the first years of our church, a family moved to our community with a severely handicapped son. After their first visit, our pastor went to "mug" them as part of our follow-up strategy for first-time visitors (more on this in Chapter 4). During the visit, the family told him that although they had enjoyed the service, we could not be their church home. When the pastor probed further, they said our church was too small to minister to them as a family because of their son's special needs. The family talked more about what might be needed, and when the pastor came back to the church the following Sunday, he asked the congregation if we would be willing to do "whatever it takes" to be their church family. We mobilized our little church to develop a ministry that would allow the family to worship weekly and attend Sunday school, while their son received personalized one-on-one care.

Today "Matthew's Ministry" is a thriving ministry of our church. Many of the children reached over the years have grown into adulthood and are now ministering back to the congregation in a variety of ways. One way is through a new bakery they started called the "Sonshine Bakery," in which they bake pastries to sell in our café and other local coffee shops.

Because we did "whatever it takes" to reach out to some visitors so many years ago, we now have a weekly ministry that serves over one hundred families in our community. We knew there was a need for that kind of church, and if we could become it, we would reach people in our community that no one else was reaching.

What About Your Church?

What is good and unique about your church? Sometimes it's easy to see the things that are not so good in our churches and miss the things that are good. Everyone reading this book has seen people leave the church because all they could see was what was not good about it. Every year this happens in our church, and it always hurts when someone leaves because their eyes were focused on the things we need to work on. But think about how you view your spouse or friends. If all you focused on was what you didn't like about them, you would have split from them years ago. There is no way to sustain a relationship if the starting point is dislike. People stay connected because they look for the good things in each other and thank God for those things. They look beyond the negative or help try to bring positive change.

Several years ago a woman visited our church and decided after several visits to join. She had just moved to our area, so I asked her how she learned about our church. It turned out she had told her neighbor that she was looking for a church and wondered where the neighbor went, thinking she would visit. But her neighbor had a curious answer: "Oh, you wouldn't like my church. But I have heard good things about Church of the Resurrection. You should visit there." Obviously, you don't want your members to say that about your church. You want them to say, "Oh, this is where I go to church, and I love it! Here are the things I love, and here's why you should come with me to my church."

Pastors and leaders, this is very important: Part of your job is to help the people in your congregation believe in your church—not just in you, but in your church. Boost the congregation's self-esteem. Help them name and claim the amazing work that God is doing and will do in your church. Give them language to articulate why it is such a great blessing to be counted as a member.

As parents, we can relate to the importance of helping our children have self-esteem. My husband and I made it a priority to find ways of helping our children believe in themselves and see their potential. When our son was in fourth grade, he had to spend ten minutes each day writing in a journal as part of his school curriculum. In one journal entry he wrote, "I love my dad because even when I don't think I am hitting the baseball very good, he tells me I am doing a good job and that he is proud of me. This gives me confidence when I am up at the plate and helps me believe in myself." Our son didn't make it to the major leagues, but he did play four years of baseball in college. The ways in which my husband intentionally shaped our son's self-esteem helped our son see his potential. In this same way, you need to help shape your church's self-esteem and enable it to see its potential.

What is the potential of your church and its ministries to your community? In what ways are you helping your church see that it is remarkable? Are you proud and excited to be serving in your church? When a church begins to believe in itself, amazing things can happen.

Armed with self-esteem, convicted and persuaded that people need Jesus Christ, need the church, and need your particular church, you are ready to put the *Catch* principles to work and go fish for people.

(To read more about Adam Hamilton's responses to the three questions, look in Chapter 1 of his book *Leading Beyond the Walls*, Abingdon Press, 2002.)

To Think About

In this chapter, you considered three important questions:

- Why do people need Jesus Christ?
- Why do people need the church?
- Why do people need your particular church?

How would your leadership group answer each of these questions? How would you? What might your answers suggest about your church's culture and ministry?

Check Point:
Looking Inward

You have reached the first of two "check points" in the *Catch* Program Guide. This is a good place to stop and debrief as a leadership team. Sit around the table or divide into smaller groups and talk through what you've read in Chapters 1 and 2.

Use the worksheet below or on the DVD ROM to process what you've learned and plan for what's next. You may want team members to read and respond separately before the discussion, or you may prefer to have the group do the exercise together as a team.

1. When you read the story in Chapter 1 about the leadership team wanting to keep the church just the way it was, how did you respond? How does it relate to your church's experience? Do you think most people want everything to stay the same, or will your members feel comfortable with the changes that new people might bring?

2. Watch the video segment titled "Relentlessly Outward Focused" on the *Catch* DVD ROM (found in the back of this book). List all the ways that your church is currently outwardly focused.

3. Describe the ways your church may be too inwardly focused.

4. Describe your church community. Would you say it is more thriving or more dying? Why? Who are the lost or wandering-off people in your area? What would it take to reach them? Who are the new people moving into your area (even just one)? A new teacher at school? A new doctor or nurse in the community health clinic? What would it take to reach them? What changes would be needed in your church?

5. In order to become relentlessly outward focused, your congregation will need to understand its purpose and know it by heart. What is the purpose statement of your church? Does it reflect an inward or an outward focus? Do you need to change or update your current language to include an outward focus?

6. Look again at the two diagrams in Chapter 1. What kind of church will you be? One that is inwardly focused, or one that is constantly casting the net wide to help those outside the church experience a personal, life-changing relationship with Jesus Christ? What might happen in your community if your church functioned like the second diagram?

7. What will be required of your church leadership in order to move from being inwardly focused to outwardly focused? What change do you anticipate being the hardest for your church members?

8. Watch the video segment titled "Three Important Questions" on the *Catch* DVD ROM. Now it's time to answer these questions for your church.

• Why do people need Jesus?

- Why do people need the church?

- Why do people need your particular church? What is unique about it?

9. In what ways will a relentlessly outward focus and a new clarity about why you need Jesus and the church provide a foundation for beginning an invitational evangelism ministry?

10. Dream together about your church. What will it look like when its members are gathering for worship, fellowship, and discipleship and then are sent out to reach people with the love of Jesus Christ? How will your leadership team communicate this dream to your congregation?

3. Attracting People in Your Community

3.
Attracting People in Your Community

As Jesus walked beside the Sea of Galilee, he saw Simon and his brother Andrew casting a net into the sea—for they were fishermen. "Come, follow me," Jesus said, "and I will send you out to fish for people."
—Mark 1:16-17 (TNIV)

My father-in-law is an avid fisherman. He has learned that certain bait attracts a certain type of fish, but not another. He loves to fish in the local lakes in our area, which are teeming with catfish, perch, crappie, and bass. Stinkbait, breadballs, and even a simple worm are tasty treats for catfish or a perch. But if you want to reel in a bass, he'll tell you that none of these options is effective. To catch the attention of a bass requires a live minnow or a shiny spinner lure. Crappie also like minnows, but not in the same way as the bass.

In order to catch a bass, the minnow or lure is cast toward the shore in the shallow water where the bass feed. To catch crappie, you cast the minnow deep in the water and keep it still until the crappie takes notice. Experienced fishermen know that one single style of bait is not effective at attracting the variety of fish in a particular lake or body of water. You need a tackle box filled with a variety of baits, lures, and weights.

As churches, one of the keys to becoming more effective at reaching people in our communities is to increase the number of tools in our evangelism tackle box. What techniques do you use to communicate about your church to those in your community? Too often, a church uses one style of reaching people—maybe a weekly ad in the newspaper, maybe a Yellow Pages ad, maybe the sign in front of the church. All are good methods, but alone they are not enough to attract the various people in your community.

In the Scripture quotation at the beginning of this chapter, note that the fishermen Jesus called were not fishing for hobby or sport; it was their livelihood. They fished to survive. Too often, churches view evangelism as important but not as their livelihood. When churches regard evangelism as the very thing that keeps them alive, it becomes more than important; it becomes essential. Beautiful sanctuaries, well-organized kitchens, and annual picnics are important, but our identity as churches depends on our commitment to effectively fish for people. We fish to survive.

When my church began, we had no building and no sign because we were meeting in rented space each weekend. We were not visible in the community, so we had to rely on a variety of methods to spread the word about our church and attract people to the weekend services. We used many different types of bait from our tackle box—phone calling campaigns, direct mail, newspaper ads, word of mouth.

Here are a few examples of communication techniques that have been used effectively in our church and others. As you read, think about the community around your church and how you might apply one or more of these ideas to fish for people in your area.

Phone Campaigns

Evangelism requires you to connect on a personal level with the people in your community. We found that one way to do this was to conduct a phone campaign allowing us to speak to as many people as possible.

We purchased a crisscross directory—a phone book arranged by street address—that enabled us to identify people to contact in a specific demographic area. We set up a phone bank, and over the course of six evenings we made phone calls to the households from the list. Using a script (see a sample on the DVD ROM), callers first asked the person if he or she was actively involved in a church. If the response was no, the caller would ask if we could send information about our new church.

About six hundred of the six thousand households contacted responded that they were not involved in a local church and would be willing to receive additional information. We then followed up with personalized letters about the church. This telemarketing method resulted in a database of six hundred households, totaling close to 1,800 individuals who had identified themselves as either non-religious or nominally religious, exactly the group we were trying to reach!

Of our charter households, many were first made aware of the church as a result of this initial phone outreach. Telemarketing is not always well received in today's society; however, if done properly and respectfully, it can be a very effective tool in your evangelism tackle box. You may say, "But we are not starting a church." Conducting a phone campaign can still be effective as a way of reconnecting with those in your church who have become disengaged, or to connect with those in the community surrounding your church.

Once you've made an initial contact with those in your area, that doesn't mean the research is over. You must continually analyze your surroundings. Use marketing surveys, lists and research as a way of keeping informed about your community and identifying those you are trying to reach.

For example, when apartment complexes began rising up around our central campus, we acquired results from a study that told us those living in the apartments would primarily be singles in their thirties and forties. This research was a catalyst for us to launch a singles ministry that eventually reached thousands in the community. We purchased a mailing list targeted at singles within five miles of the church. We sent a direct-mail piece inviting them to the church, letting them know that if they did not have a church family, we would love to be theirs. When they arrived at our church, we very intentionally tried to speak language that would include them—for example, avoiding language that applied only to families or married couples. We also made certain we had great programming and ways for singles to connect quickly.

People who enjoy fishing know the value of research. They rely on reports by experts who analyze local bodies of water and provide important information about fishing conditions and about the species of fish that are biting—where, when, and on what bait. Time spent analyzing this research aids the fisher's quest for a productive day of fishing.

Churches can also benefit from research. Besides a crisscross directory, other data sources specific to your community include your local school district, chamber of commerce, and various planning and community action committees, just to name a few. You may discover other resources available in your community.

Direct Mail

Direct mail has always been an important and effective outreach tool for connecting with people in the community. Our church, following the phone campaign, designed three direct-mail pieces aimed specifically at attracting the unchurched rather than luring members from other congregations. Each piece articulated our vision, including an invitation to join us for worship, and was sent to approximately 10,000 households from a purchased marketing list.

When we held our first worship service, close to 120 of those in attendance were from the community. Almost all had heard about the church from either the phone campaign or the direct mail piece. We continue to rely heavily on direct mail to get the word out about the church. Direct mail actually becomes more effective the longer it is used, because many people respond only after receiving mailings for two or three years.

Adam Hamilton offers this advice about direct mail:

> Do it well, do it positively, do it regularly, and send it to thousands of households. Doing it well means that the quality, the concept, the artwork, the paper, and colors should all be sharp. A poorly designed mailer can do more harm than good. I suggest having the senior pastor and one or two talented graphics or marketing people design the piece. It should not be designed or tweaked by committee. The piece will lose its edge and effectiveness if too many people are a part of the design process. Doing it positively means that your message should be a positive one; negative messages tend to turn unchurched people away (though the people in your church may like them). Doing it regularly means sending out mailings two to three times per year for several years. Direct mailing has a residual effect; many respond only after the fourth, fifth, or sixth mailing they receive. Finally, direct mail works on the "law of large numbers." Your response rate for a well-designed direct mail piece might be only one-tenth of one percent; if you send out three thousand pieces that might indicate that as few as three to as many as ten households would visit. Often the response rate is much higher, but be prepared for a rate within this range. (*Leading Beyond the Walls*, 36-37)

Direct mail is an important evangelism tool even if you are not launching a new church. Send direct-mail pieces for special events such as the opening of a new building or an open house after a renovation; for Vacation Bible School, parenting classes, or senior adult programming. Send direct mail sharing your desire to be a church for children and teenagers by highlighting the programming you have available.

We also send approximately three direct-mail pieces a year, most often in the form of a postcard, inviting people to worship. One typically goes out in August, as families are finishing summer break and preparing to go back to school; and our two largest mailings are invitations for Easter and Christmas Eve worship services, when non-religious and nominally religious people often consider going to church. These postcards offer a personal, compelling invitation to attend worship.

Another strategy is to print extra copies of any direct-mail postcard and provide them in the weekend worship bulletins. We are very specific with our members, telling them that the postcard is not for them; instead it should be used to invite someone. We ask members to pray for a friend, co-worker, or neighbor who does not go to church, then deliver the postcard personally, inviting that person to attend worship. The combination of the prayer, personal invitation, and printed postcard is very persuasive in getting people to visit.

As you begin to think about direct mail, what message about your church do you want to communicate to the community?

Candlelight Christmas Eve

Think about the high-attendance times of your church year. If you took a survey, most churches would probably say that Christmas and Easter are the most-attended services. Our growth at Church of the Resurrection has, in large part, been driven by our Candlelight Christmas Eve worship services. These worship services are designed so that when visitors come, they feel welcomed and understand what is happening in the service. We offer the highest quality worship experience possible, with great music and a sermon designed for new people who do not necessarily know Christ, helping them understand what Christmas really means. By offering multiple worship services, we make sure that all those who attend for the first time on Christmas Eve will have a seat when they arrive.

History tells us that a first-time visitor will most likely attend either the 7:00 or 9:00 p.m. service on Christmas Eve, so these services take a more traditional form, with hymns that the visitor may have sung as a child or young person. Because we know these services will be the most heavily attended times, and because we want to ensure that all our visitors have a seat, we ask our leaders and church members to worship at one of the services being offered at other times, leaving seats available for first-time visitors during the two popular service times.

For the less popular times, we design services with a specific target in mind. For example, we have a service designed for those who enjoy contemporary music, one for senior adults that includes an old-fashioned Christmas sing-along, one for families with young children that includes a shorter sermon and other worship elements designed specifically for children. Finally, we offer an 11:00 p.m. service designed to conclude at midnight (Christmas Day) with Communion. All these services end with the powerful passing of the light, in which the sanctuary is darkened and then gradually lit through the passing of a flame from candle to candle and person to person.

Every year we receive e-mails from people who tell us that they gave their lives to Christ for the first time during a Candlelight Christmas Eve worship service. The image of Christ entering a broken world and piercing the darkness with light is brought to life in that transformational experience on Christmas Eve.

You may not have a need for multiple service options, but it is very important to view the Christmas Eve service as an invitational evangelism opportunity. Your sanctuary will be filled with members and their out-of-town guests, as well as those in your community who may not know why they always go to church on Christmas Eve—they just do. Here is your chance to connect with these visitors and open them up to the life-changing love of God that comes to us through Jesus Christ. Don't waste an opportunity to reach this group of people!

Fishing Expeditions

Because we have identified Christmas Eve and Easter as high-visitor-attendance times, we are intentional about not only communicating the love of God during those services, but also inspiring visitors to return. For this reason, we always announce a new series of sermons scheduled to begin right after the holiday. We make certain that the sermon series speaks directly to the questions and concerns of an unchurched person. We call these sermon series "fishing expeditions," drawing from Jesus' invitation to the disciples to become "fishers of people." The fishing expeditions are specifically aimed at addressing the question, "What would unchurched people want or need to hear in order to come back to the church?"

Think about how you could follow up a Christmas Eve worship service or other high-visitor-attendance Sunday with a "fishing expedition." Imagine what would happen, for example, if you announced on Christmas Eve, "Starting next week, we'll have a sermon series asking the question: Why do bad things happen to good people? You've wrestled with prayers that weren't answered. You've seen things happen that you couldn't reconcile with a good and loving God. If you ever wrestle with these questions, we'd like to invite you back for our next three sermons on 'Where Was God When?'" If you announce that series of sermons on Christmas Eve, I guarantee that your members will want to come, and so will your non-religious and nominally religious visitors.

Other examples of fishing expedition topics include series on marriage, parenting, Christianity and world religions, Christianity and science, and controversial issues. Additional topics can be found in worship and small group studies, at local bookstores, and at the Church of the Resurrection Web site, www.cor.org. As you implement the *Catch* program, sit with your team and brainstorm ideas.

You may also want to survey your congregants. Each year our senior pastor e-mails the congregation, inviting them to help him think about sermon topics for the upcoming year and to discern what God would have him preach. In the e-mail he asks that each person pray for guidance, then respond to the following questions:

1. After Christmas and Easter, we plan a sermon series that will be of very strong interest to people who attend Christmas Eve or Easter services but who don't usually attend church. What ideas do you have for a sermon series that would be easy to invite your unchurched friends to?
2. Throughout next year we will preach several sermon series focused on helping you grow in your faith. What suggestions for topics or practices do you have for specific sermon series aimed at helping you grow in your faith? These could be sermons on a particular book of the Bible, on specific biblical characters, on practices of the

Christian faith, on questions of Christian theology, or on some other dimension(s) of the Christian life that would help you in becoming a deeply committed Christian.
3. Each year we prepare a couple of sermon series focused on pastoral needs many of us have—a sermon series on forgiveness is one example. Consider the personal struggles you or those you love face. What are the practical life questions or concerns you think should be addressed in an individual sermon or a series of sermons?

When our senior pastor receives the responses, he takes time to read and pray over each response, ultimately creating a one- or two-year preaching plan based on this input.

Newspaper and Radio Advertising

Although we have determined that direct mail is one of the most successful ways to attract first-time visitors, there are other effective methods. One is newspaper advertising. We advertise each week in the faith section of the local paper. Although most non-religious and nominally religious people will most likely not be reading the faith section of your local newspaper, we maintain this weekly ad because we find that people who are moving into the area or are visiting the area will look here as a source to find a local church to visit. Even with the prominence of the Internet and the ability to research information more readily available, we continue to monitor the effectiveness of newspaper ads. We realize there may be a time in the near future when this form of advertising will no longer reach people effectively.

You can also take advantage of your local community event calendars. Most of these are free, so you can share dates for programs you feel would be attractive to the community, such as parenting classes, senior adult fellowship events, community service opportunities, or special guest speakers.

Stories written about church members or features about your church can also attract visitors. Each fall we host a 5K walk/run called Sacred Steps. The proceeds from the event fund ground-level projects in sub-Saharan Africa to overcome the devastation caused by HIV/AIDS. Before one of these runs, a young woman read the story about our event. She did not attend church but loved to run, so she made a decision to participate. She became so excited about the mission that she became the largest fund-raiser and has since become active in the church.

We have had articles written about our neighborhood food drives, our Christmas Eve services, and our work with inner-city schools. We even have had articles written about our sermon series. One summer we did a sermon series titled "Going Fishing," in which each week's sermon highlighted fishing tips from a professional bass fisherman. This caught the attention of a local sportswriter, and he wrote an article about the sermon series in the sports section of the newspaper.

We also strategically purchase advertising space on a local secular radio station primarily for invitation to Christmas and Easter services. Notice that the advertising is on secular radio, not Christian, so we can connect with unchurched people who would not be listening to Christian radio. We create sixty-second ads aimed at teaching a parable that might connect with an everyday life question or experience. Here is a sample script from one of the spots that ran during the Christmas season:

The Gift on Behalf of Others

> Are you looking for some last-minute gift ideas? Can't decide what to give someone who has everything?
>
> Hi, I'm Adam Hamilton, Senior Pastor of the Church of the Resurrection. A friend recently gave me a great Christmas gift—a share of a sheep that was donated to a family in a third-world country. I recently gave someone else a gift of ten meals provided in his honor to those who are homeless in a shelter here in Kansas City.
>
> If you're looking for a great gift to give someone who has everything, consider giving a gift in their honor to someone who has nothing. A gift of $10, $20, or $50 to area agencies that work with low-income people can make a difference and be a great way to let your friends and family know that you care about them, and you care about others.
>
> If you'd like help finding a way to give this kind of gift, check out our Web site at www.cor.org where you can find links to area agencies and suggestions and opportunities for how you can work directly with them to give gifts that really will make a difference.
>
> And, if you don't yet have plans to attend a Christmas Eve Candlelight service, I'd like to invite you to join us for one hour—one hour that will help you remember what Christmas is really all about.

Consider this for a moment: Unchurched people will only visit a church if they know about it. If they are not aware of your church, how can they find you? Particularly during Christmas and Easter, when a non-religious or nominally religious person might be motivated to attend worship, it is important to have a strong, noticeable presence in your community. As any good fisher knows, you may not always catch a fish in your favorite fishing hole each time you visit; but if you are persistent, you will eventually reel one in. Although newspaper and radio may not be the most effective forms of attracting visitors, they do provide additional ways to make your presence known. Consider all approaches to share the message about your church and what it offers to the community.

Web Site

The Internet is becoming an increasingly important tool for evangelism. If you have sent out direct-mail pieces and placed radio and newspaper advertisements telling people about your church, they will more than likely visit your Web site first before they decide whether to "bite." For many, that series of clicks will be their first visit to your church. Knowing this, our church is committed to organizing information on the homepage with a first-time visitor in mind, including a prominent place where visitors can sign up for a weekly e-newsletter. Because this e-newsletter has links embedded in the articles, we have found it is our primary driver back to the Web site, not only for our members but for visitors as well.

The homepage of your church Web site should be designed with an easy navigation system tied to your vision, purpose, and mission. Visitors should easily be able to read more about your church, find worship times, and locate directions. We post a video about the upcoming sermon series and offer video links for people to watch the past week's sermon. Consistency throughout the site makes it easy to move among pages where a visitor can view, read about, and register for any event online. If you want your site to be helpful to visitors, make it easy for them to contact someone for additional information or to ask a question.

What does your Web site communicate about your church? Does the site make your visitors feel welcome? Is it easy to navigate? Or is it full of outdated information that sends people away in confusion and frustration?

Social Media

As the church, we are called to be where people are, and Facebook and other online communities are places where people today interact. You may think that your church doesn't need to be in the world of social media, but you can be sure there are people in your community who can be reached through these avenues.

Facebook is an online space that allows individuals to connect personally with the lives of friends and families. Companies have also found Facebook an invaluable resource to reach customers and potential customers. Facebook provides a free avenue for connection and allows for greater interactivity than a static Web site. A church Facebook group gives you immediate communication with much of your congregation, and any updates you make on your page may show up in your members' news feeds, giving your church free publicity. Having a presence on Facebook can facilitate connections among church members and make it easier for current attendees to invite their friends. Consider setting up a page that provides basic information about worship time, updates on events, and opportunities to engage with others.

Twitter is another excellent source for immediate updates, news, prayer requests, and invitations to events. Twitter provides a service in which people or organizations respond to the question "What are you doing?" in 140 characters or less. Churches can use Twitter to provide updates, called "tweets," on what is happening in the church and opportunities to be involved. Because it is possible to "retweet" a message, spreading a received message to a group of followers, Twitter is a great tool for evangelism. Churches can provide updates that can be spread virally through circles of influence to communicate good news. Not long ago, our church posted information about an upcoming opportunity. Within two seconds, responses of interest were already being received, and the information was being retweeted, casting the net to an even greater circle of people.

If you are intimidated by the thought of using social media, ask around in your church and find out who the local social media expert is. Don't be surprised if it is a high school student! Ask the person to set up a Facebook account for your church and invite all the members. Make sure any information about location, worship times, and upcoming events is public information that can be viewed by anyone. Have your expert set up a Twitter account and teach you how to send tweets. You should attempt to send out several tweets every week for maximum effect.

Community Events

Your building itself can be bait that lures people to the church. Because we recognize that the building is an important evangelism tool, our church has been intentional about opening our doors to the community and allowing it to be used for outside events. For some people in the surrounding area, their first experience of the church may be participating in a community blood drive, college graduation, symphony concert, school district teacher training, Boy Scout meeting, homeowners association meeting, or other community event. We make sure each person who comes to our church feels welcomed and comfortable, no matter why they are coming (more on this in Chapter 4).

Weddings and funerals provide an incredible opportunity for evangelism. During a wedding you have the opportunity to reach people for Christ and help give spiritual direction to a family for generations to come. Hundreds of people who have joined our church indicate the first time they visited was attending one of our weddings. A wedding that is done well not only blesses the bride and groom but also creates an opportunity to reach guests who may not have been in church for years. Likewise, a wedding done poorly will reinforce for those same people all the reasons they do not attend church (see *Leading Beyond the Walls,* pp.117–18.)

As with weddings, we have had hundreds of people begin to attend Church of the Resurrection after a memorial service, who eventually became members. Every memorial includes people who may not darken the door of a church at any other time, at the very time when they are wrestling with truly important questions about death, the meaning and purpose of life, how we understand God's love in relationship to evil and suffering, and so much more. A well-led memorial can move persons to reconnect with God and return to your church. The key is being present with the family and taking time to develop a meaningful ministry experience through the memorial (see *Leading Beyond the Walls,* p. 124.)

Word of Mouth

Direct mailing, newspaper and radio advertising, the Web site, and social media are all important tools for attracting visitors; but often the most effective evangelism method is personal invitation. Evangelism happens best through relationships, when people get excited about their faith and invite friends along for the journey. Research has shown that unchurched people are more likely to visit a church if they are invited by someone they know—neighbor, close friend, co-worker, family member. Over 90 percent of those who join Church of the Resurrection tell us they first visited because someone invited them. That is why we provide tools to our church members, such as sermon-series postcards, so they can more effectively "fish for people." Our hope is that these tools will help to break down barriers of intimidation and fear as people reach out into the community.

In addition to sermon-series postcards, we have found technology to be a useful tool, and we have developed an e-vite for each of our sermon series. There is a shared link on our Web site where church members can go, type in e-mail addresses for those they would like to invite, and write a personal message of invitation. The e-vite is sent with the personal message and a link to a video promotion about the upcoming series and an invitation to church.

We also supply pocket testaments to our members and encourage them to find a few extra minutes wherever they are to open the pocket testaments and start reading. We challenge members to get "caught" reading their Bibles, then give them away. Like the sermon postcards, these pocket testaments are not for them but for people outside the church.

Finally, we have discovered that preaching is the most effective bait that attracts visitors back to worship. All the other tactics may get visitors through the door, but the sermon is what will bring them back. Our goal is for our pastors to preach sermons that share the good news and invite people to respond. Our senior pastor has been quoted as saying, "My job is to be the tastiest worm possible."

Evangelism is helping people hear the good news of the gospel and motivating them to respond. A variety of efforts must be made to persuade others of their need for Jesus Christ. Make known, through the methods shared above, the ways your particular church can help meet this need, and do so in a way that inspires, motivates, and invites them to respond.

How good is your congregation at attracting and inviting people to come to church? How effectively are you inspiring and helping your congregation to invite their friends? How intentional are you about reaching out to unchurched people in your community, then attracting and persuading them to come in?

To Think About

In this chapter, you considered ideas and methods for outreach, or marketing:
- Phone campaigns
- Direct mail
- Candlelight Christmas Eve
- Fishing expeditions
- Newspaper and radio advertising
- Web site
- Social media
- Community events
- Word of mouth

What methods is your church already using? How effective have they been? What methods are you not using? Which of these methods are you equipped to do, and how helpful do you think these methods might be?

4. Making Visitors Feel Welcome

4.
Making Visitors Feel Welcome

Offer hospitality to one another without grumbling.
—1 Peter 4:9 (NIV)

Each year my family spends a week during the winter in Destin, Florida. For a Midwesterner, time in the Florida sun during the winter is a treasured experience. One of the favorite activities for my husband and son is to fish from one of the local jetties with my stepfather and brother-in-law. They love getting up early in the morning, packing lunches and snacks, and making a day of it. I look forward to enjoying their prize catch of grouper, red fish, and trigger fish.

During one of these fishing adventures, my brother-in-law and stepfather decided to catch grouper by using shrimp as bait. They settled in on the jetty and baited their hooks with the shrimp. Within seconds my brother-in-law's pole dipped deep into the water, signaling the bite of a fish, and then his second pole dipped. Wow, what excitement! He spent the next few hours attracting and catching fish after fish. My stepfather, on the other hand, was not getting a bite. What was going on? They were fishing in the same location, with the same bait. Finally, in exasperation, my stepfather asked my brother-in-law what he was doing to attract so many fish. He discovered that my brother-in-law had taken an extra step in preparing his bait. My stepfather had been putting the shrimp from his bait bucket right on to the hook, while my brother-in-law had taken time to peel each shrimp carefully, apparently making it more inviting to the fish.

Growing churches understand that attracting first-time visitors requires attention to detail, doing the extra things. According to research, visitors will decide in three to eight minutes whether they will return. If during that brief time they form a negative impression of the kind of church you are, they may never have an opportunity to see your strengths.

A first-time visitor begins formulating feelings about your congregation before getting out of the car. These impressions are formed by: the appearance of your facilities and grounds, the quality of your signage, the congestion in your parking lot, the friendliness of the congregation, the cleanliness of your nursery, and a long list of factors.

Having now considered strategies to invite people into church, your task is to pay attention to the details so that your building, people, and programs work together to create a positive first impression.

Every time a visitor walks through the doors of your church, an opportunity unfolds. This individual has taken the time to worship with you for some reason. Look at every first-time visitor as someone who may be genuinely unchurched, for whom this may be their first time in years to visit a church. The visit may have taken a great deal of courage, or may be in response to a great need they are currently facing in life. Often visitors come only after a friend has invited them five or six times, or after having received one of our mailings seven or more times. Since this is likely the case, we want to do everything in our power to help visitors feel the welcome of Christ and to motivate them to return the following week.

Recently we asked our trustees to tour the church facilities with the eyes of a first-time visitor. They were given digital cameras and asked to take a picture of anything they saw that would not be attractive to visitors. They discovered poor directional signage, peeling paint, stained carpet and ceiling tiles, potholes in the parking lot, unsightly landscaping, and nurseries that were difficult to access. These pictures were used to create action steps for correction, and over the following year we addressed each issue. When was the last time you took a look at your building and programs from the perspective of a first-time visitor? Let's look at some steps you might consider taking to transform your church into a welcoming environment.

Signage

When visitors approach your building, do they know where to go? It can be hard to imagine their perspective if you've been in church all your life, but take a minute to look with a visitor's eyes. Do you know where to park? Do you know which entrance to use? Do you know where to go once you're inside? Appropriate signage puts visitors at ease and points them exactly where they need to go. It is also an indicator that you are expecting visitors and that you have prepared for their arrival.

The largest signs on the outside of your building should direct people into your main gathering space and sanctuary. Such signs will put new people at ease and help them know immediately that they are in the right place. The longest walk for a visitor is from their parked car into your building. Great signs help point the way and communicate: You are welcome here.

Interior signs should direct people to specific locations such as classrooms, restrooms, nurseries, check-in locations, the information desk, and the sanctuary. All signage should be visible and easy to read. A few years ago our church opened a beautiful children's educational space. We had intentionally spent time making sure each room was clearly labeled so families would know where to take their children. However, we hadn't considered that when the hallways were filled with people, the signs would not be visible. We had beautiful signage, but it couldn't be seen! We spent the next month ordering and redoing the signs, putting them perpendicular to the wall and above the doorway, clearly visible to all.

Have you ever entered a church where doors or walls are cluttered with leftover tape from old signs or covered with information about different meetings or events? What did this look like to you? What did it communicate? What kind of first impression did it create? If your doors and walls look like that, consider getting some inexpensive floor sign holders that use standard copy paper. Then you simply print the information you want to communicate and insert it into the sign holder to get a polished, professional look.

Also consider providing signage for people who may be coming to the church for events other than worship, such as weddings, funerals, community events, and classes. We use portable outdoor signs to welcome these guests and to provide directions for parking that put them closest to the entrance where the event is being held. These signs are inexpensive and can be purchased from most printing or office supply stores. They are weatherproof and make use of metal stands that are easily used and moved. Let visitors know you planned for their arrival.

Visitor Parking

A few years ago, my family and I visited a large church in Dallas, Texas. Having read about the church, we were excited to visit. When we arrived, the parking lot was congested, and we saw three large buildings. People were streaming into all three buildings but because there was no outdoor signage, we weren't able to tell which was the main worship center. After circling the lot several times, we finally found a parking space toward the back of one of the lots. We entered the building closest to where we had parked, only to discover it was the children's building. It was a secure area, so we had two options: go back outside and around to the main sanctuary, or use some outer hallways to wind our way through the building until we came to the main foyer. We decided to go outside. When we finally reached the sanctuary, we discovered that the doors were closed because the worship service had started. After the opening welcome, prayer, and songs, we were allowed in, but as a result of our experience we felt unsettled and anxious. There was no doubt we were outsiders.

If you want your church to be outwardly focused, make sure to welcome visitors from the minute they pull into the parking lot. Reserve parking spaces just for them. By providing these reserved spots, you can strategically assign parking-lot greeters to welcome them. As visitors enter the parking lot of our church from the street, we have signs inviting first-time visitors to turn on their hazard lights. By doing this, they can be directed by parking lot greeters to spaces we have reserved especially for them. These spaces are located close to the building, with quick and easy access into the sanctuary.

We have discovered that many first-time visitors are the last to arrive for worship, so providing parking spaces close to the building gives them easy access and helps them get inside more quickly, with less anxiety and stress— one more detail that demonstrates we are expecting them, and they are welcome.

Parking Lot Attendants

One of the first personal touches our visitors receive is from our parking-lot greeter ministry. This team serves several purposes. They greet first-time visitors in a specially designated area and answer any initial questions. In addition, they keep the traffic moving so people can enter the parking lots quickly, efficiently, and safely. Trying to find a place to park can be stressful for many, and this team helps eliminate this stress by keeping the traffic flowing smoothly.

When we first launched this ministry, some people wondered who would sign up to stand in the parking lot in the rain, wind, cold weather of winter, and brutal heat of summer. But, our senior pastor cast a compelling vision of the ministry's importance, calling people to be on the front lines welcoming our visitors and caring for our congregation. This is now one of our strongest and most dedicated teams. They arrive early to serve each week, no matter how bad the weather is. They begin by checking to make sure the parking lots are free of trash and clutter. Then, following a team prayer, they stand in their assigned parking lots smiling, waving, directing traffic, and providing care for all who arrive.

Greeters

Another way to make a good first impression with visitors is to have greeters at every entrance to your building. These greeters give a warm welcome to all who enter, and their enthusiasm for the church can set the tone for the entire visit. Greeters reflect the love of Christ by being welcoming, hospitable, and gracious to all who enter. They wear specially marked greeter nametags, clearly identifying who they are. They provide direction, not by pointing the way but by personally walking with visitors to the place they are looking for. Greeters are attentive to people who may need special assistance, such as the elderly or a family with infants and young children.

Greeters need training that includes how to be friendly without being overly so. The goal is to welcome people but not to overwhelm them. A good way to do this is by offering an outstretched hand and simply saying, "Welcome to our church. We are so glad you're here." Greeters should be trained to welcome children as well, not just adults. One family in our church confided that the moment they decided to join the church was when the greeter not only greeted them but also bent down and greeted their children, eye to eye. To the visiting family, it was a sign that this church valued and welcomed children.

With greeters in the main gathering places in your church, it is easy for their friends to come up to them and begin talking. However, when visitors see others huddled in conversation, they may feel that they don't belong. We tell our greeters that if a friend approaches while they are greeting and begins an extended conversation, they can say, "I'm serving right now and will be finished in fifteen minutes. I can't wait to hear more. Let's meet after service to catch up." By attending to details such as this, you can make sure your visitors will receive the attention they deserve.

Nametags

Do you remember the old sitcom *Cheers,* set in a local bar where people gathered for friendship, fellowship, and conversation about life? If you do, I'm sure you also remember the opening theme song that describes a place "where everybody knows your name." Names are important, and greeting one another by name forms community.

People gather in church each week to find friendship, discuss life, and experience fellowship with others. To remove the pressure from remembering names, print nametags for all your members, volunteers, and staff. You can even offer nametags to regular visitors if they so desire. These provide an easy way for people to call each other by name, making connections more personal. It is more meaningful to offer Communion to a person as you look them in the eye and call them by name, or pray for them by name, or greet them after the worship service by name. Disposable stick-on nametags can be made available for visitors. Take care, however, not to have special nametags that single out visitors. Everyone wants to be welcomed, but being singled out can be uncomfortable. Churches that offer radical hospitality know the difference.

We place bulk orders of clip-on nametags with our church name preprinted on them from a local office supply store. Using clear labels and a label machine, we are quickly able to make a personalized nametag for anyone who requests one. Bulk ordering allows us to take advantage of quantity discounts.

We encourage members and staff to wear their nametags to all church events and gatherings. There are many inexpensive options for nametags that can be found online or at your local office supply store; your local discount store may carry nametag-making options. Being able to greet someone by name is the first step to building a relationship and is a great way to create a culture of friendliness.

Clean Facilities

Visitor-friendly churches pay attention to details, especially when it comes to the overall cleanliness and appearance of the facility.

One of our staff members was recently asked to visit a neighboring church and give some first impressions. When he arrived, he saw that dogs had gotten into the outdoor trash bins and had spread trash all over the grounds. He also noticed that the grass had not been mowed. When he went inside, the church foyer was cluttered with mission donations, and the reception desk was covered with old papers, out-of-date brochures, and items from the lost-and-found. These first impressions began to tell a story about the church.

In his drive to the church, he had noticed many homes with outdoor swing sets and children's toys, so he asked to see the church nursery. As he walked in, he smelled dirty diapers and mildew, masked with a faint scent of Lysol. The ceiling tiles were stained, toys were broken, and the rooms were poorly lit. When asked if he would like to see the sanctuary, he said, "I don't need to, because if I were a first-time visitor with small children, I wouldn't feel safe leaving them in your nursery, and I would not be back."

Dynamic churches are constantly on the lookout to see how they can improve. At our church, we have made major strides in keeping our gathering area free of clutter by designating spaces for missions collections, lost and found items, and coat storage. We have set times throughout the day when the bathrooms are cleaned and restocked and the trash is picked up. We touch up paint and have a regular cycle for replacing stained ceiling tiles. We also ask that our mowing crews come on Friday of each week, so the grass looks well-kept and manicured for weekend guests.

Enlist the help of your leaders. Ask them to pick up trash when they see it. Suggest that after washing their hands in the restroom, they wipe down the sink and dry it with a paper towel. These are little things, but they can make a big difference. We don't always get it perfect, but we are constantly asking the questions: What can we do to create a more welcoming space for visitors? Does the condition of our facility honor God? Does it say that we believe what we are doing here is important? Does it demonstrate quality and caring?

Visitor-Friendly Worship Service

When your efforts to attract visitors begin to bear fruit, you will find first-time visitors in worship regularly. Teams will have welcomed visitors from the parking lot to the foyer, creating an environment where the visitor begins to feel comfortable. You will have transformed your space into a welcoming place where no one feels like an outsider. And now, the worship service itself should reflect the same welcoming concepts. Worship is the place where visitors should most feel that they belong. But for many, it is the very place they feel like outsiders.

I have spent time in Eurasia facilitating leadership development seminars and working with church leaders. During the worship services, I find myself confused as to when I am to stand, sit, pray, sing, or simply listen. This is in part because I don't understand the language, but it may also be the way a visitor feels during worship in your church. People who don't usually come to church may not know the words to common liturgy, beloved hymns, or prayers. They may not know if they are to stand for the reading of Scripture, kneel for prayer, or how to take Communion. To address these issues, go out of your way to make sure visitors understand what's going on during worship, and don't assume they will know your cues.

At Church of the Resurrection, our aim is to offer worship for our congregation that is a blend of Scripture, tradition, experience, and reason. We don't want to sacrifice our identity to make sure newcomers feel welcome. Rather, we want to help them understand what we do in worship and why we do it.

The key to helping first-time visitors fully engage in worship is to interpret, explain, and adequately set up each element so they can understand the service and feel comfortable participating. Here are a few ideas of how we attempt to make sure our first-time visitors are engaged and not left feeling that they are on the outside.

Welcoming Announcement

When it comes to the beginning of worship, whoever speaks first sets the emotional and spiritual tone of the service. We always have a high-energy person deliver the welcome. If you don't want a low-energy service, do not have a low-energy person give the words of welcome. We begin worship each week with these words, "Welcome to The United Methodist

Church of the Resurrection! We are so excited that you are here today! My name is _____, and we are so grateful that you have chosen to worship with us today!" The introduction of the worship leader or pastor by name is important. Without this introduction, a first-time visitor wonders, "Who is this person?" Can you imagine inviting a visitor into your home and not introducing yourself? This is one small way to welcome visitors—tell them who you are before you lead your part of worship.

Greeting Time

In several churches I have visited, I've been given a special nametag to wear because I am a visitor, or I am asked to stand at a certain point in the service to be recognized. At our church, we are careful not to make our visitors stand out. We do not give them special visitor nametags or make them rise to be recognized. Most visitors do not wish to be recognized or called out, but they do want to feel that someone noticed they were there and was friendly and welcoming toward them.

Immediately following the words of welcome during worship, we invite the members of the congregation to stand and greet one another. Our worship leader will say, "Let's take a moment to welcome one another. Sitting around you may be people who are visitors. There may be someone sitting next to you who had a very difficult week and just needs to feel the warmth and encouragement of another. With that in mind, let's welcome one another." The energy level in the room goes up immediately. At times, we will invite people to tell those around them how long they have been coming to the church, or where their hometown is, or some other bit of information that encourages a sense of connection and sharing. This helps to build community and lets visitors find a connection point before worship begins.

Attendance Notebooks and Information for Visitors

After the opening hymns and prayer of confession, we pass an attendance notebook down each row to record attendance while the pastor says, "I invite our ushers to come forward and hand out the attendance notebooks. If you would, please sign in and let us know that you are here; we would be most grateful. As you are signing in, take a look to see who is sitting next to you and welcome those persons by name after this service of worship. If you are a visitor, the information on the left-hand side is there for you to take so please help yourself. Once the book is at the end of the aisle, please pass it back to the beginning of the aisle so the folks on the other side can see who you are." The left side of the notebook includes several brief flyers about the church. Visitors quickly recognize this as one more indication that we anticipated their visit.

Explaining Each Worship Element

We don't assume that visitors understand the transitions between the opening hymns, prayers of confession, baptisms, Scripture readings, sermon, or offering. We want our visitors to feel welcomed at each point in the worship service.

At the beginning of worship, we offer words of instruction to help set expectations for what will happen in the service. The welcoming pastor says, "We have gathered here to worship God, to sing praise to God's name, to lift up our prayers for thanksgiving and confession. We've come to lay before God our concerns. Our hope is that God will speak through the music, the reading of Scripture, and the message so that we might know God's will for our lives. We hope you will leave renewed and refreshed and ready to serve God in the world. With that in mind, let's take a moment to pray." Then, during the opening prayer, the pastor may invite the congregation to lay their hands on their laps, open palmed, and to repeat a prayer line by line such as, "Lord, help me to set aside all the thoughts that compete with you for my attention. Help me to worship you with my lips and with my heart." Or, we may simply offer a similar prayer on the congregation's behalf and then, with enthusiasm, the pastor will say, "Let's stand together and worship the Lord."

We project the words to the songs, the Lord's Prayer, and any special reading or liturgy on our screens, or we print them in the bulletin. We don't assume that people know the words to any of the liturgies, prayers, praise songs, or hymns. When we participate in the sacraments, our pastors give words of instruction as a way of helping everyone feel included.

Connection Point

The Connection Point is located in our main gathering space. It is our central location for high-level customer service. Trained volunteers serve at the Connection Point with direct access to the church computer system, allowing them to access information, register people for programs or events, answer questions, provide directions, and send e-mails to ministry connectors for follow-up. We also keep visitor packets at the Connection Point. Visitor packets contain ministry flyers, a letter from our senior pastor, an audio CD of a sermon, and a map of our campus. We include the audio CD in the packet rather than a DVD, in hopes that visitors will play it in the car as they leave and listen to it immediately.

Coffee and Refreshments for Fellowship

After we have set up an environment of welcome from our parking lot to the sanctuary, we maintain this same sense of welcome by locating coffee and tea stations throughout our narthex area. Coffee and refreshments create a sense of fellowship and hospitality. These stations encourage people to linger after worship to visit and connect with others. Even before we had our coffee café, we used rolling utility carts with sixty-cup coffee pots or catered in coffee from a local grocery store.

Making Room for Visitors

From the beginning, we've made sure to provide open seats for visitors, and our ushers are trained to be attentive and look for them. We have discovered that visitors often arrive last to the sanctuary; and, if your congregation is like ours, your members tend to sit toward the back and on the aisle, leaving the middle sections of each row open. So, where do visitors have to sit if they arrive late? In the front—after they have crawled over the people sitting on the aisle to get to their seats.

We try to be proactive and avoid this situation on behalf our visitors. First, we ask that the ushers constantly survey the room for open seats so that when visitors arrive, they can quickly be seated. Second, at the beginning of the service the worship leader will invite people to move to the middle, making room on the aisles for those who may arrive late.

Also, let's consider briefly how many people your building can hold. Let's say your sanctuary seats one hundred fifty people. You already know that the usable capacity of the room is actually lower. The sanctuary can hold that many from time to time, but if it is filled every Sunday, eventually the attendance will drop. Why? Because when a room is overcrowded, visitors begin to think, "Well, that was enjoyable once, but I don't think I want to go back again. It was just too crowded." You will also discover that people will stop inviting their friends, figuring that the sanctuary doesn't have room for them. So, as a general rule, your usable capacity is about eighty percent of the total. If your sanctuary can seat one hundred fifty people, you are really full at one hundred twenty.

Think about how you can increase your capacity to welcome new people. You may decide to do so through additional services or a new building project. Ideally, make the best use of the facility you already have to create room for new people.

Caring for Children

When it comes to connecting people with your church, the children's ministry may be one of the most important types of bait in your tackle box. During its early years, our church attracted many families with children. At that time, I was serving as our children's ministry director and I jokingly would say, "Our pastor is the bait that brings people in, but our children's ministry is the hook that keeps them." It was said in jest, but there was some truth to it. Parents will only leave their children where they feel each child is safe, and, in our age of consumerism, where they believe their children are "having fun." We made it a priority to develop a children's ministry that was engaging, interactive, safe, family-centered, and, yes, fun, all while guiding children on their journey to know, love, and serve God.

The safety of children should be of the highest priority. No matter the size of your church, a well-organized check-in and check-out process is important. Design a procedure where children can only be released back to a parent or designated caregiver. We currently use a computerized bar-scan system that matches child and parent, but in the past we have used a number system, matching nametags, and other processes to match up child to parent.

In addition to safety, we have also been intentional about creating an environment for children that is engaging by using bright colors, age appropriate toys and activities, and interactive experiences. You want children to enter the space and say, "Wow!" the way they do when arriving at their favorite pizza place or theme park.

Creating a "Wow!" space does not have to be expensive. Enlist creative volunteers to use their gifts and talents in evaluating and upgrading your space. You will be surprised at the difference simply changing the paint color will make—for example, from "church taupe" to something brighter and more vivid.

Caring for children is not just about paint choices and great toys, however. Those who serve as greeters, Sunday school teachers, and leaders are most influential to the first impression a visiting family receives. Help your volunteers understand the important role they play in attracting and connecting children and their parents to your church. Their energy, level of engagement with each child, and love for the children will make a huge difference.

We have repeatedly found that as children connect with their leaders and the other children in their classrooms, they are the ones who get their parents out of bed for church on Sundays. They absolutely do not want to miss out! Your pastor may spend hours preparing excellent sermons; your parking lot team may have done an incredible job of welcoming people as they arrive; but if parents are not satisfied with the experience their children have, many simply will not return.

Receptionist and Voice Mail

One final note on transforming your church into a welcoming environment: Remember that some impressions may not be made in person. Be sure your phone receptionist is one of your most highly trained and enthusiastic team members.

Phone receptionists are your front line, and at our church they are responsible for the highest level of customer service. Church leaders are required to keep phone receptionists informed about current programs and ministry, plus any new opportunities for members and visitors. In addition, these receptionists stay up-to-date with staff schedules so they can best direct incoming calls.

When the receptionist is not able to answer the phone directly, voice mail serves as your information system. Arrange voice mail so the incoming caller can get pertinent information first, and then make sure there is a helpful menu for additional options. We include worship times and a list of staff extensions as the first options available.

Positive first impressions are critically important in attracting first-time visitors to consider a second visit. This is true not only for worship on Sunday, but for the children's area, adult Sunday school area, and all other points of contact.

Little things matter. Have you taken time to discover the little things that need attention at your church?

To Think About

In this chapter, you considered ideas, methods, and roles for making visitors feel welcome at your church:
- Signage
- Visitor parking
- Parking lot attendants
- Greeters
- Nametags
- Clean facilities
- Visitor-friendly worship service
- Welcoming announcement
- Greeting time
- Attendance notebooks and information for visitors
- Explaining each worship element
- Connection Point
- Coffee and refreshments for fellowship
- Making room for visitors
- Caring for children
- Receptionist and voice mail

Discuss among the leadership group how well your church is doing in these areas. What areas could be improved, and how? What might you do personally to help the church improve in one or more of these areas?

5.
Connecting and Following Up With Visitors

5.
Connecting and Following Up With Visitors

Share with the Lord's people who are in need. Practice hospitality.
—Romans 12:13 (NIV)

This past winter I was in Russia facilitating leadership training for pastors and lay members. The subject of fishing came up in a casual conversation. A pastor asked me, "Do Americans really make fishing a sport where you catch fish and then release them?" I was a little surprised by his question because I had never really given much thought to this aspect of the sport—where the fisherman works hard at attracting the fish using all the right bait, only to release the catch. When I told the pastor it was true, he responded, "Why would a fisherman work so hard to catch something and then just let it get away? When we fish, we go with the intention of keeping the fish."

His comments made me wonder about our churches. In what ways do we attract new visitors to the church but, without effective connection and follow-up strategies, let them get away? We have explored strategies to attract visitors to your church. We have talked about the importance of paying attention to details and creating an environment that welcomes visitors. But what happens next? Growing churches have effective follow-up and connection strategies.

At some point during the year, most churches will have first-time visitors. Every time they walk through the doors of your church, an opportunity unfolds. The question is: How will you follow up to encourage those visitors to come back? What will you do to help them experience the welcome of Christ through your church and motivate them to return the following week?

I recently joined a health club for the first time. I had received postcards and information in the mail for more than a year from this particular fitness center. I had driven past it every day on my way to and from the church office, had seen the building and sign, and had overheard my co-workers talk about how much they enjoyed working out there. Finally I got the courage to try it out. Going for the first time was an effort for me. I felt intimidated. I didn't know how to use the equipment, and I was concerned everyone working out would be much more advanced than me. I would be the outsider.

Mustering all the courage I had, I walked through the door. I was greeted by a friendly trainer who acquainted me with the machines and helped me get started. I had a good experience on my first visit and great intentions of returning. I know that working out is something I need to do, but that was over two months ago and I have yet to return. And, no one at the health center seems to have missed me, as I have not received any follow up from them. So, each day when I drive by the facility on my way to work, I think that I really should get back, but I keep driving.

I believe many of our first-time visitors find themselves with this same feeling after they visit our churches. They have a great experience and believe that attending church is important, but for some reason they lack the motivation to return.

Effective follow up offers encouragement and motivation for the visitor to return for a second, third, and fourth visit. It is among the most important things you will do if you are serious about reaching the unchurched in your community.

Mugging

You may remember from the previous chapter that during worship at our church, we take time to find out who is visiting. During the service, while the special music is playing, we invite the ushers to hand out attendance notebooks. Everyone, including visitors, signs in.

We know that some visitors don't want to give their name and address. However, when the pastor asks the people sitting next to them to look and see who they are and to welcome them by name, it becomes more of a challenge. We don't want to make this a high pressure situation, but the information in those notebooks informs how we connect and follow up with visitors and members, so it is important to us. After several years of handling sign-in this way, we have discovered that most visitors will decide they want to be greeted and will happily sign in.

After each worship service, the attendance notebooks are collected. A team of volunteers inputs the weekend attendance information so that we know exactly who was in worship and who was absent. If any of our members misses, one of our volunteers contacts them personally. We want our members to know they are missed. Taking attendance is time-consuming, but it is very important for the effective care of the congregation.

Not only do the attendance notepads help us keep up with our members, they also let us know who is visiting for the first time. The attendance notebooks have two forms—one for members and the other for visitors. By having these two forms, we are able to prioritize data entry. When the notebooks are collected following each service, visitor information is given to an onsite volunteer data entry team that immediately inputs the data into our system.

After the information is entered, we use online mapping tools to print out directions to the visitors' homes. These maps are inserted into a coffee mug that contains information about our church. The mugs are placed on shelves by zip code or neighborhood, and after each worship service a team of volunteers committed to a particular area picks up the mugs and delivers them within forty-eight hours.

Knocking on the doors of these people, the volunteers say something like this: "Don't worry. I don't want to come in. But I wanted you to know how glad we are that you and your family visited our church today. Thank you so much for coming. I have a small gift for you; this is a coffee mug with our church's name on it. We would like you to have that as a gift. And we want it to be a reminder that we would love to be your church family. There is a little more information about our church inside. Do you have any questions?"

If there are no questions, the volunteer says goodbye and leaves. If the visitor isn't home, the volunteer writes a personal note, puts it inside the mug, and leaves it by the door. The visits don't take long at all, and a coffee mug isn't something that gets easily tossed out. Every time that visitor opens up the kitchen cabinet, he or she is going to see our church name there on the shelf.

We use a specialty printing company to supply the mugs. Each year we select a theme to imprint on the mug, which also includes the name of our church and the year. When we first started the church, we would order extra mugs and sell them to our members for up to twice the actual cost of the mug. Our members loved having the current year's mug, and they knew that by purchasing the mug they were helping to ensure that a visitor would get one. Currently, we purchase mugs as a part of our annual stewardship drive. Each family that makes a commitment to the annual stewardship campaign receives that year's coffee mug as a small token of appreciation. The rest of the mugs are used for first-time visitors.

If coffee mugs are not in your budget, consider a gift of bread, cookies, a candle, or something else to say, "Thank you for coming." Following up with first-time visitors needs to be a priority for your church in order to grow and thrive.

Third Visit Follow-Up

After visitors have come to your church three times, consider taking another step to connect with them. Have a church leader—or better yet, your senior pastor—make a home visit.

During the first five years of our church, our senior pastor, Adam Hamilton, would personally phone individuals or families after their third visit. He would contact them and thank them for visiting the church and ask if he could drop by their home for thirty minutes. He would use this time to get to know the individual or family more, share his personal faith story, and give information about the church. At the close of the visit, Adam would pray for them. For many of these visitors, it was the first time someone had prayed aloud for them as an adult.

During that visit, we usually became the person's church family, because Adam had taken the time to listen and to develop a relationship. He may not have led them to Christ yet, but he had begun a relationship that would lead them toward Christ. In the first five years of the church, Adam made five hundred visits such as these. Only one of those families didn't join; all the rest joined our church.

When asked about the most important thing he did to help the church grow in the first five years, Adam always answers, "Delivering coffee mugs and doing in-home visits." This is still the most effective means of bringing visitors to Christ.

Church consultant and author Bill Easum reinforces the importance of the senior pastor's personally handling this first-time visitor follow-up in his article "How to Grow a Church Under 500 in Worship" (see *http://www.transformingchurch.com/resourcetoolbox/2007/11/how_to_grow_a_c.php* [accessed 9.26.11]). Easum writes,

> So you can begin, pastor, by making in-person calls on first-time visitors within twenty-four hours after they attend and 85 percent of them will return the following week. If this home visit is made within seventy-two hours, 60 percent of them return. If it is made more than seven days later, 15 percent return. You see, the average person today visits several churches before deciding on a church home. This means they may not come back for six weeks. By then, they decide which church to return to by the friendliness and helpfulness of the members. If you wait until they return the second time, you lose 85 [percent] of your visitors.

The Connection Point

Easy access to information about your church is important to a visitor. Having a central location is an effective way for visitors to quickly spot where they can get information on weekends. We call ours "The Connection Point."

We have found that some visitors come in during the week to get information, so we keep the Connection Point staffed with a volunteer not only during worship but also on weekdays. We want to make certain we are able to connect with as many people as possible. These weekday volunteers may be at the information desk all day and never speak to a person, but they commit to do it because they understand the importance of being there that one time when a person does enter the building.

The Connection Point volunteers are well-trained. They know the history of the church and are prepared to answer many basic questions about ministries and programs. They know how to access information from the Web site to answer questions, and they also know how to contact a ministry leader or staff person to get additional information if needed. Ministry brochures are attractive and displayed so that they can be found easily. All brochures are written to reach a non-religious or nominally religious person, someone new to our church and its ministries. When asked directions to a class, program, or event, our volunteers make sure to walk the visitor there instead of just pointing the way.

Each of our church ministries seeks ways to connect with visitors easily and quickly. In adult discipleship we launch new classes, small groups, Bible studies, and service projects regularly so that a person never has to wait very long to get connected. Our children's and student ministry areas also have easy, ongoing entry points. Assimilating into the life of the church as quickly as possible is a key to retaining visitors.

For all inquiries, timely follow-up is given a high value at our church. We ask all our staff and ministry leaders to return phone calls and e-mails within twenty-four hours. We also make sure to use out-of-office messages on voice mail and e-mail so that anyone who contacts us is able to know when a follow-up reply might be expected.

A plan for effective follow up is critical if you are going to cast the net wide and retain visitors. The plan needs to go beyond a form letter in order to be personal and authentic, helping you to connect relationally with your visitors.

God genuinely cares about your visitors, and I can think of no greater motivator to inspire excellent follow-up and connection procedures. If I were to visit your church for the first time this Sunday, do you have a plan to follow up with me and help me get connected?

To Think About

In this chapter, you considered ideas and methods for connecting and following up with visitors:
- Mugging
- First-visit response
- Third-visit follow-up
- Connection Point

How good a job is your church doing to note, respond to, and follow up with visitors? What are some ways you could improve?

6.
Inviting Others to Grow in Faith

6.
Inviting Others to Grow in Faith

But grow in the grace and knowledge of our Lord and Savior Jesus Christ.
—2 Peter 3:18 (NIV)

I had the blessing of growing up within close driving distance of my great-grandparents' two-hundred-acre farm in southwest Missouri, deep in the Ozark Mountains. During visits, my great-grandfather would grab his cane fishing pole and I would follow him to the pond for an afternoon of fishing. During those fishing trips, he would invite me to sit on the bank of the pond while he baited his hook with one of the big earthworms we had dug up in the garden and put in an old coffee can.

He would fish, and I would watch. I watched how he baited the hook; I watched how he cast the line in the pond; I watched how he noticed the action of the red bobber; and I watched how he reeled in the fish. I did a lot of watching. One day, after many visits to the pond, he handed me a baited hook and said, "I want to teach you to fish." He was calling me to move from sitting on the bank of the pond to a higher level of participation.

We have a tendency to allow our congregants to sit in the pew weekend after weekend listening to great sermons, but not calling them to a higher level of participation. We don't invite them to take the next step of commitment in their walk with Christ.

In Mark 1:16-20, Jesus invited some fishermen to follow him and learn to fish for people. He called them to a higher level of commitment—to be disciples—to leave behind what they had known, follow him, and be fully active in ministry.

We must find ways to inspire people to move from their pews and take the next step. Why were the fishermen sitting on the seashore observing what was going on around them?

Maybe they, like many in our congregations, were waiting for a specific invitation, a tangible next step.

Too often, we list activities in the church bulletin to point out ways that people can be involved. We expect them to initiate the next step and seek additional information on their own. And truthfully, if we were to evaluate those activities, would they genuinely lead to a deepening relationship with Christ? How much thought have we given to a clear discipleship path, one that can be easily understood and followed by a non-religious or nominally religious person?

To guide people on their journeys of faith, we must create clear and easily understood paths of discipleship—paths starting where people are and guiding them on their spiritual journeys. Just because an activity or program is hosted by the church does not in and of itself make it transformational. We need to evaluate our programming constantly and ask the question, "How is this event, this program, this Bible study helping people on their journeys to become deeply committed Christians?"

At Church of the Resurrection, we always look for ways to help people take the next step. There was a period in the life of our church when participation among members and new visitors decreased. This was perplexing. We had more programs than ever, more Bible studies, more opportunities for people to participate in. Why were we seeing a decrease in the number of people who were involved? When we asked people why they had not taken the next step, most responded, "I am overwhelmed. There are so many choices, I just don't know what I want to do."

We quickly realized the importance of designing an intentional discipleship path with clear next steps, and then communicating it effectively. This strategy is critically important, no matter how many members or programs your church has.

Invitation to Join

For us, it begins with inviting a visitor to join. The threshold to become a member of the church is low, but we set high expectations for membership.

After a person has visited the church three times, personal contact is made, as described in Chapter 5. A letter or an e-mail is sent, inviting the person to an event at the church called "Coffee with the Pastors," where he or she will learn about membership and be invited to join. A public invitation is printed in the weekly worship bulletin; weekly e-mail communication is sent; and announcements are made from the pulpit. The invitation is for anyone who is interested in learning more about the church or how to move from being a visitor to joining the church and becoming member.

As the visitors arrive, they are greeted by a team of volunteers who serve as hosts. Each visitor is provided with a nametag, a folder of information on the church, and a membership form. The information folder contains a simple, well-worded brochure about the church and what we believe; stewardship information, including a commitment card; and specific information about next steps in discipleship and connection. We do not include information on every ministry program, but instead only provide information about the recommended next steps, with the hope of inspiring them to connect immediately.

During these events, our pastors share their stories of how they came to faith in Christ and how Christ has transformed their lives. They share the story of the church, so that visitors can better understand the church's purpose and vision, and what we believe God is calling the church to be in the future. They also describe what membership in the church represents.

At the close of the event, we invite those attending to become members. If they decide not to, we tell them they are welcome to visit as long as they would like, and we will still be their church family. We will visit them when they are sick and in the hospital; they can participate in church ministries, Bible studies, and programs; and they can serve. We will do their funerals and weddings, and we will pray for them. But if they decide to join, they will be making a commitment to fulfill the membership expectations.

Membership Expectations

Some churches downplay expectations for new members, fearing that visitors will be turned off by requirements. At our church, we believe the opposite. We think people are looking for something to commit to. We think they want a place to belong. We see membership as being similar to a marriage; it's a sign of commitment. People understand that when you get married, you must bring something to the relationship as well as get something out of it. In the same way, when you commit to a church through membership vows you feel responsible for the church and commit to its purpose, vision, and ministry.

So, we're clear from the very beginning that with membership there are expectations involved. For instance, when visitors become members they will no longer be able to park in the spaces close to the building set aside for visitors. They will receive the annual stewardship mailings, including a pledge card. They will be held accountable to serve inside and outside the walls of the church. We will check their worship attendance and contact them when they have missed.

Many times, this part of the discussion moves visitors toward membership. They want their membership to mean something. They want to become more committed to Christ and the church. The fact that membership is about responsibilities and expectations, not just privileges and benefits, makes it all the more compelling.

Specifically, we have four expectations of membership:

1. To worship regularly.

Members are expected to attend worship every weekend unless they are sick or out of town.

2. To continue to grow in their faith by participating in a small group study.

Members are expected to grow in their faith apart from worship. We have developed an intentional discipleship pathway to help guide them toward a small group. Members are also encouraged to read Scripture and pray daily as a way of growing in their faith using a daily resource we have developed called the GPS: Grow, Pray, Study guide. The GPS is a daily Scripture reading based on the weekly sermon, with short devotional questions and an insight prepared by one of our church leaders. It is available in a daily e-mail, on our Web site, or as an insert in the worship bulletin.

3. To serve God with their hands by volunteering in service to the congregation, the community, and the world.

Members are expected to serve God at least once a month within the walls of the church, and a minimum of ten hours per year outside the walls of the church. God has called us to be salt and light in the world, and one way we do that is by serving others and sharing Christ. We have entry-level opportunities such as a monthly FaithWork, when an individual can simply show up to serve for two or three hours with no additional commitment, or to sign up for a one- or two-month commitment such as ushering or greeting, all leading an individual toward a higher level of commitment.

4. To give in proportion to their income.

Members are expected to give according to their income, with the tithe being the goal. Commitment to generosity is an important step on the journey to know, love, and serve God. The Bible teaches us to give a tithe, or the first 10 percent of what we earn, to God and God's work. We understand that 10 percent is a goal for some and a starting point for others. We explain to prospective members that when they return a portion of their resources to God, they are investing in God's vision and mission, and they create an opportunity for God to work through them and the church.

Recognizing that it is human nature to become complacent, each year our senior pastor preaches sermons aimed at reminding members of the church's expectations and inspiring them to take the next steps to grow in faith and commitment to Christ. In addition, all our program ministries clearly communicate how a person's participation in that particular ministry or program is helping them grow in their faith.

The Joining Service

After membership expectations have been described at Coffee with the Pastors, there is a time of prayer. During this prayer, visitors ask for God's guidance and try to discern whether this is the church God would have them join. After prayer, there is a ten-minute break for coffee, lemonade, and cookies. Various ministries leaders are on hand during the break to answer questions.

After the break, those who have decided to become church members are invited back for a joining service. For those still undecided, we remind them we will still be their church family, and they are welcome to return and join at a future Coffee with the Pastors.

The brief joining service includes reciting the Apostles' Creed and answering the following questions:

- Do you wish to be a disciple and follower of Jesus Christ?
- Will you make this your church family, allowing the people of this church to love and care for you, as together we serve God with our prayers, presence, gifts, service, and witness?

At the conclusion, we officially welcome them as members. New members complete the membership paperwork, and we take their pictures to include with their information in our database. At times, we have also posted these pictures with the family's name on a bulletin board in a prominent location in church. It is important that not only our pastors and staff have the opportunity to meet them but that the congregation be given a chance to welcome them as well.

The weekend following Coffee with the Pastors, we announce how many new members have joined and invite them to stand during the worship service. Our senior pastor explains that the people standing have made a commitment to become church members. In return, he asks those who are already members to make a commitment to be their church family, and the congregation responds, "We will." We then offer a prayer of thanksgiving for the new members.

We take two additional steps to help the congregation get acquainted with the new members. At the beginning and end of worship, we scroll the new members' names on the video screen, and we list them in the weekly e-mail to the congregation. Everyone is encouraged to look through the list for someone they may know and to welcome them personally, and we invite the congregation to pray for each new member by name during that week.

Discipleship Pathway

The Christian life is not meant to be lived alone. We were created for connection—with God and with one another.

By now you have considered ways to invite non-religious and nominally religious people into your church. You have read about the importance of a purpose statement, against which everything you do can be measured. You have thought about and discussed outreach strategies, attention to detail, and a commitment to do "whatever it takes." You have learned about worship services designed to connect with unchurched people and the value of radical hospitality. And you have read about follow-up strategies and ways to invite people into a greater commitment.

But what is the end goal? Where are we taking people? Each church's answer might be slightly different. At Church of the Resurrection, we have defined deeply committed Christians as those who know God with their mind, or are being theologically informed; love God with their heart, or are being spiritually transformed; and serve God with their hands, or are working and representing Christ in the world. We call this approach "Our Journey: Knowing, Loving, and Serving God."

We recognize that each person, whether visitor or member, is at a different place on the journey. We know that each day, people are faced with decisions, demands, and converging pathways in which they must decide what is most important and what direction to take. We don't want their faith journey to be too complicated, so we have developed a simple pathway to help connect people easily on the journey to know, love, and serve God. We want them to say yes to the amazing journey God has planned for them!

For many, worship is that first step. But for others, it is service. We have found that many first-time visitors have actually participated in one of our community service opportunities before ever attending the church. Imagine what might happen if your church became known as the place where anyone in the community could find a way to serve others, whether by painting a school, serving a meal, joining a house renovation team, or sewing school uniforms for children in Africa.

While volunteering at one of our urban school partners, I met a young man who was painting in the same room. I asked how long he had been attending our church. He replied,

"Oh, I've never been to your church. In fact, I don't go to church. My friend told me that you were working on this painting project, and I thought it sounded like a good way to give back to the community. That's why I'm here, just because I want to make a difference." Several weeks later I saw the young man at worship. He told me he was curious about the church and had decided to give it a try. Since that time, he joined the church and became actively involved. More and more, we are finding that it's through community service that we are connecting with first-time visitors.

As you implement some of the ideas and strategies in *Catch,* you may want to begin conversations about how to engage with more people by offering opportunities for them to serve in the community and the world.

After connecting with visitors through service or worship, you have a great opportunity to invite them to consider a next step. For occasions such as this, it is important to develop an intentional discipleship plan. A busy church calendar filled with many programs may or may not be intentional. It may just be "busy." Evaluate each of your offerings and ask, "How is this program or event helping people grow in their faith?"

Journey 101 and Beyond

One way to develop an intentional and effective discipleship pathway is to offer a staged series of large-group and small group experiences. At our church we call these Journey 101.

Journey 101 courses are designed to provide an introduction to the essentials of the Christian faith. In these classes we discuss what it means to fully know, love, and serve God. Each class is designed to be a combination of large-group teaching with small group conversations. Using information we receive from registration, we create table groups made up of individuals with similar affinities, such as stage in life or hobbies or service interests.

Currently we have four Journey 101 offerings. The first is a three-week introduction that each person is encouraged to take. Then, after a ten-week overview of the Christian faith using the international Alpha program, we offer three six-week classes, each exploring in more depth what it means to know, love, and serve God.

Knowing God

This class explores the good news of the Bible and helps participants discover study tools and resources to deepen their understanding of Scripture. More than two-thirds of those who take the class are non-religious or nominally religious people, with no basic knowledge of the Bible, how it is organized, or how to use it; so we offer this basic Bible class to set a foundation for faith formation.

Loving God

During this class, we introduce participants to spiritual practices that will help them grow in their relationship with God and others. Each session focuses on a different practice, and each participant leaves with a practical way to experience that practice during the week.

Serving God

In this class, an individual discovers what it means to serve God with their resources of time, talent, and finances. We also cover the basics of evangelism and faith sharing.

Because we believe one of the best ways to nurture a growing relationship with Jesus Christ is to belong to a small group of Christian friends who encourage, challenge, and support one another, we have a team dedicated to helping our congregants find a small group best suited for them based on where they live, their interests, or their life situation.

For those who are not ready for a small group because of personal or emotional issues, we provide a pathway for them to experience authentic Christian care and connection through one of our support groups or the national Celebrate Recovery ministry. Through worship, fellowship, teaching, connection with others, and caring facilitation, they experience the love of Christ leading them to wholeness and healing. Ministries such as Divorce Care, Grief Support, Celebrate Recovery, and other support groups also serve as incredible outreach ministries, attracting people in the community who do not have a church home.

The goal of an intentional discipleship pathway is to guide communication so that next steps are clear and are not overwhelming or confusing to the individual. You are inviting people to become a part of something bigger than themselves, to take the next step on a journey toward a deeply committed relationship with Christ.

Jesus' disciples didn't hesitate to follow him when he called them from the shore. His message must have been so compelling that there was no way they would pass up this journey of a lifetime. Our churches should inspire people to drop everything and follow Jesus. We can implement all the effective techniques and have visitors pouring through our doors, but if we don't inspire them to take the next step, what have we really accomplished?

We are all on this journey together. It's important that visitors and new members understand that we share the journey no matter where our starting point is—whether as children who are learning to know, love, and serve God in their own way; teenagers who are beginning to unleash their faith in God; or adults at various stages in their lives. Our invitation is to begin the journey toward a deeply committed relationship with Jesus Christ.

How are you calling visitors and non-engaged members from the "shore" and inviting them to discover more about following Jesus?

To Think About

In this chapter, you considered methods, steps, and approaches involved in inviting visitors to join your church:
- Invitation to join
- Membership expectations
- The joining service
- Discipleship Pathway
- Journey 101 and beyond

Does your church have a clear and inviting path to membership? What does the church expect of members, and is it communicated clearly? What can you do personally to bring visitors into the church family?

Check Point:
Moving Outward

Now that you've read the final section of the Catch Program Guide, explore the state of inviting, welcoming, and outreach ministry in your church. Determine where change is needed, and plan for action.

In this section you have learned about attracting, connecting, transforming, and helping visitors along their journey. As a leadership team, debrief the major ideas presented in the section and dream together about what might happen if you put some or all of these ideas into practice in your congregation.

1. Think about direct-mail and other strategies. How might traditional public relations methods attract and connect you to non-religious and nominally religious people in your community?

2. View the "Strategic Marketing" segment from the DVD ROM. Take some notes as you watch. How do you think the following techniques could lead people to your church? Note any church members who may have related experience or be gifted in these areas.

- Geography—Determine your target radius.

- Lists—Decide what kind of database of household addresses you need for your strategy and plan.

- Direct Mail—Determine a few times a year when you might use a direct-mail piece.

- Phone Campaigns—How might you use a crisscross directory to help you connect with people in your community?

- Newspaper and Radio Advertising—Where will you place your ads? In the faith section of the newspaper? in the calendar? How will you get stories written about your events?

- Web Site and Social Media—Evaluate your site. Is it user-friendly? Is first-time visitor information prominent? (This includes worship service times, locations, a calendar of events, contact names and numbers, links to additional information.)

Ask a local student to help you set up and maintain a Facebook page. Discuss the most effective ways of using social media.

- Word of Mouth—How will you help your members feel comfortable handing out postcards announcing an upcoming sermon series, or business cards with your church's information? How will you encourage them to hand out pocket testaments?

3. As you dream of getting the word out about your church and its ministries, what is the one thing you most want to communicate about your church? How effective are your current efforts to communicate that one main idea you want people to have about your church?

4. As you think about creating a welcoming environment in your church, use the chart below to help you evaluate what your visitors currently experience. Identify action steps for improvement, and suggest a person or team of volunteers to lead the change.

Element	Current experience	Action step to improve	Person or team
Outdoor signage			
Indoor signage			
Identified visitor parking and greeting			
Well-trained greeters			
Nametags			
Well-maintained facilities			
Information area			
Coffee and refreshments			
Care for children			
Receptionist			

5. Now think about your worship service from the viewpoint of a first-time visitor. Do you feel like a stranger in a strange land, or do you feel welcomed and relaxed? View the DVD ROM segment "A Welcoming Worship Environment." Use the chart below to evaluate your current level of welcome. Identify areas where you can improve, and suggest a person or team to lead the change.

Element	Current experience	Action step to improve	Person or team
Well-trained users			
Seats available for visitors			
High-energy welcome			
Introduction of worship leaders by name			
Greeting time			
Attendance notebooks			
Information available for visitors			
Explanation of the worship elements			
Printed words to songs, prayers, and liturgy			
Sermons that connect with the unchurched			

6. View the DVD ROM segment "Connecting and Following Up With Visitors." Why is follow up important? Discuss the ways in which your congregation is good at connecting

and following up with visitors, and think of ways in which you could improve. Consider starting a "mugging" ministry or some equivalent. What value could it serve in your particular situation?

7. Create action steps. Now that you have learned about specific ideas related to connection and follow-up with visitors, consider ways in which these ideas might translate into action steps for your church. Here are a few questions to get you thinking:

- How will you collect visitor information? If you use an attendance notebook, who will design the notebook and attendance sheet?

- How will you maintain attendance data on your visitors and members? What type of software system will you need? Who can help to set it up so it can be integrated with your membership data? Who will input the data and maintain it on a weekly basis?

- How will you follow up with first-time visitors? What tools will you need to help with this follow-up? (Consider first-time visitor gifts such as coffee mugs, personalized letters, visit scripts for volunteers, and so on.)

- How will you follow up with third-time visitors? What will you invite them to do?

- Do you have a new-member event such as Coffee with the Pastors, so that visitors can consider their next steps? If you don't, design one. Here are some suggested guidelines:

    * Make the event or class personal, offering great hospitality. Consider the setting, such as an in-home visit or a gathering at the senior pastor's home or church fellowship hall.

    * Share the vision and purpose of the church in a way that is compelling and inspiring.

    * Help individuals take their next steps as they commit to becoming followers of Jesus Christ.

8. How do you feel about setting expectations for members? If you were to set expectations, what would they be?

9. Where are you leading people? Do you have a clear pathway for discipleship? Why is having a clear plan important? What new classes or service opportunities might you start so that new people can connect into the life of the church quickly?

10. What other tools can you think of that would help you close gaps and connect with every single visitor who walks through your doors, or that would help you keep members engaged?

11. Go back through your action steps and note any church members who might be a good fit for leading a team or volunteering.

12. You have read the Catch Program Guide, considered what it means to be outwardly focused, discussed ways to attract and connect with visitors, and evaluated strategies for following up and providing next steps. Now it's time to put your plan in motion. Use the timeline provided here or create your own. One good way to start is to launch a "fishing expedition," to begin immediately after the Christmas Eve or Easter worship service.

DVD ROM Documents

DVD ROM Contents

VIDEOS

1. Becoming Relentlessly Outward Focused (3:05)

2. Answering Three Important Questions
- Why Do People Need Jesus Christ? (1:51)
- Why Do People Need the Church? (1:34)
- Why Do People Need *Your* Church? (3:12)

3. Attracting People in Your Community
- Church Communications (3:50)
- Strategic Marketing (3:20)
- Direct Mail Marketing (4:58)
- Christmas Eve Worship Promotion (3:34)
- Careful Creative Execution (3:04)
- Newspaper Advertising (2:23)
- Dynamic Website (1:46)

4. Making Visitors Feel Welcome
- Making Visitors Feel Welcome (3:53)
- A Welcoming Worship Environment (2:57)
- Welcoming and Greeting Newcomers (1:59)
- A Welcoming Worship Experience (3:50)
- Extending a Welcome During the Service (2:29)
- Getting to Know Your Church Visitor (4:04)
- Faithful to Jesus' Command (1:59)

5. Connecting and Following Up with Visitors (6:55)

6. Inviting Others to Grow in Faith (10:22)

DOCUMENTS

Program Guide Documents

- Check Point: Looking Inward (see page 39)
- Check Point: Moving Outward (see page 95)
- Inviting the Leadership Team
- Sermon Helps and Key Scriptures
- Planning Calendar
- Program Guide—For Duplication (see DVD ROM)

Small Group Participant Book Documents

- Ministry Descriptions and Commitment Form

Implementation Guide Documents

1. Attracting People in Your Community
- Phone Script
- Ring No Answer Script
- Sample Radio Ad

2. Making Visitors Feel Welcome
- Welcoming Language for Worship
- First-time Visitor Touch Points

3. Connecting and Following Up With Visitors
- First-time Visitor Letter
- Third-time Visitor Letter

4. Inviting Others to Grow in Faith
- Email Invitation to Coffee with the Pastors
- Follow-up Letter to Coffee with the Pastors
- Sample Membership Form
- Letter to New Members
- New Member Survey

Appendix: Documents for Ministries and Planning
- Ministry Descriptions and Commitment Form
- My Ministry Commercial
- Traffic Ministry
- Greeter Ministry
- Connection Point Ministry
- Mugging Ministry
- Planning Calendar (see page 114)

Program Guide Documents

INVITING THE LEADERSHIP TEAM

Leadership in the church is not meant to be owned solely by the pastor. As Jesus was preparing to launch his public ministry, even he invited a team of twelve to join him. In selecting those he would equip to become fishers of people, he recruited some who already had some knowledge of fishing, and others were chosen because of gifts they brought to the team–courage, boldness, honesty, questioning spirit, teachability, commitment, and, for the most part, a deep willingness to do what was needed to care for others in need.

You will want a diverse group of leaders helping you implement the ideas and strategies presented in *Catch*. This program is not just designed to increase church attendance, but to help your church remember its purpose and mission to reach lost people, introducing them to the love of Jesus Christ and guiding them on their journey to become disciples committed to being part of God's redeeming work in the world.

The leadership team you select should consist of both staff and key lay leaders. Look for leaders who love Christ, who are passionate about the church and its mission, who love people, who are ready to consider change, and who have the ability to influence others. They should have enough time to participate fully in the *Catch* planning and implementation.

As you recruit your team, take time to pray. Then personally phone or meet with those you will ask to serve. You are asking for a significant commitment of time and energy, so the invitation should be personal, casting a compelling vision. A team of twelve members plus the pastor is recommended, but in any case the team should have no fewer than six members, plus the pastor, and no more than twelve.

The makeup of the leadership team will vary from church to church, depending on church size, style, current committee structure, and other factors. Here's one effective way of organizing your leadership team. You can adapt this to fit the needs of your church.

Team Leader

Your Team Leader, as head of the leadership team, will work closely with the pastor to coordinate the details of the *Catch* program. The Team Leader will manage the logistical needs of the *Catch* team, facilitate meetings, and follow up on action steps. The Team Leader should be well respected, have project management skills, be highly relational with excellent communication skills, have the ability to facilitate discussion and navigate conflict, and be able to see the big picture while managing details.

Worship Team Leader

Your Worship Team Leader will work closely with the pastor to create a worship experience that helps visitors and long-time members to encounter the living presence of God. This leader will work closely with the pastoral team, music team, and hospitality team. The leader should be creative, have excellent organizational skills, have an understanding of worship flow and liturgy, be able to lead change in those aspects of worship that exclude first-time visitors, and be able to see the big picture while managing details.

Hospitality Team Leader

Your Hospitality Team Leader will work closely with the pastor to help create an environment that is outwardly focused, not inwardly focused. This leader will recruit, equip, and schedule teams to serve as ushers, greeters, and other hospitality hosts; create a space and coordinate the details to serve coffee and refreshments before and after worship services; oversee hospitality at Coffee with the Pastors or a similar gathering; coordinate nametags; and help cast a vision for radical hospitality to be a value expressed in all the ministries of the church. This leader should have the gift of hospitality, be highly relational with the ability to recruit others, have excellent organizational and communication skills, and have a high level of energy that will be influential in other areas of the church.

Connection Team Leader

Your Connection Team Leader will work closely with the pastor in overseeing processes to help individuals integrate effectively into the life of the church. The Connection Team Leader will design and implement processes for collecting, inputting, and reporting of attendance data; set up followup processes for first-time and third-time visitors; oversee a mugging or similar ministry; coordinate an information or connection area that receives information from the ministry areas on ways to connect in discipleship and serving; and partner with the discipleship leaders to distribute the small-group materials that are part of the *Catch* program. This leader should have excellent administrative and organizational gifts; be detail-oriented; be able to multi-task and oversee multiple projects at one time; be highly relational with great listening skills and a deep passion for people and meeting their needs; be skilled at recruiting, training, and sustaining volunteers; and have the ability to maintain a 20,000-foot view of the church's ministries to help individuals connect quickly and effectively.

Facility Team Leader

Your Facility Team Leader will work closely with the pastor to maintain the buildings and grounds as tools for attracting and connecting visitors. The Facility Team Leader will guide the team to look at church facilities through the eyes of a first-time visitor, develop a facility maintenance plan, install great directional signage inside and out, create parking spaces for first-time visitors, and work with ministry teams to create a weekly cleaning and upkeep process. This leader should have a eye for detail, have some knowledge and skill related to basic facility maintenance, be able to manage a budget, have the ability to schedule and oversee project management, and help others to see the church plant as a effective tool for outreach.

Marketing and Outreach Team Leader

The Marketing and Outreach Team Leader will work closely with the pastor to develop communication tools to reach out into the community and attract new people, as well as tools that effectively reach within the church. This leader will coordinate the design of flyers and information brochures, create sermon series postcards, design bulletins, oversee mailings and advertising, coordinate the purchase of mailing lists and demographic studies, design tools that congregants can use to invite their friends, develop and maintain the church Web site, create a plan for integrating social media, and provide graphic support for the worship team. This leader should be creative, have some basic knowledge of marketing techniques, possess excellent verbal and written communication skills, be able to manage details, and have the ability to recruit, equip, and sustain volunteers.

Prayer Leader

The Prayer Leader will work closely with the pastor to insure that prayer is at the center of all discussions, ideas, changes, and new processes. The Prayer Leader will develop and coordinate a thirty-day prayer calendar; work alongside the connection team to pray for first-time visitors, new members, and other needs of the church body; coordinate other prayer initiatives as needed; and personally will pray daily for the pastor, leadership team, and volunteers, as well as for the church and your community. This leader should be spiritually mature, have good oral and written communication skills, and possess the ability to enlist other prayer partners.

The remaining members of the leadership team should be diversified in gifts, abilities, passions, influence, gender, and age. It is important to find a teenager or young adult to serve on your team, as well as representatives of the church council, elder board, and other ministry areas. You may even want to invite a person from the community to sit in on your team meetings and provide fresh perspective as an outsider. As you invite team members, encourage them to take time to pray before they accept and then follow up with them in two to three days.

You and your leadership team are getting ready to embark on an exciting journey as you cast the nets wide and move to deeper waters. This is a bold initiative, one that will require perseverance, patience, and effective teamwork. Be prepared for conflict along the way; change is hard. Some will catch the vision quicker, others a little slower, and others not at all. Be prepared for discouragement, as some ideas simply will not work the way you had envisioned. Most of all, be prepared personally for an amazing spiritual encounter with God as you commit yourself to daily prayer and devotion to this program, and corporately as a church as you begin to fully live once again into the vision and mission that God has called you to.

Jesus and his team of twelve set out together on a journey to fish for people. They experienced conflict, setbacks, frustration, and fatigue, but in the end a joy that surpassed anything they had ever known. Together they launched a movement that literally changed the world.

Maybe it's your time to launch a movement that will change your community.

SERMON HELPS AND KEY SCRIPTURES

Week 1. Becoming Relentlessly Outward Focused

Scripture
- Matthew 4:18-22 (Fishing for People)
- Matthew 9:35-38 (Lord of the Harvest)

Key Points
- Jesus calls his disciples to fish for people.
- As the body of Christ, the church is called to be Christ's physical presence in the world, searching for the lost, reaching out to them, and inviting them in.
- Jesus was relentless in seeking and saving lost people. He calls his church to be relentless in looking outward and finding ways to serve, show compassion, and lead people to Jesus.

Response
I will leave behind my fear of change and the comforts of the shore to answer Jesus' call to the deeper waters of the community.

Prayer Focus
Lord Jesus, when you called those young Galilean men to 'fish for people,' they answered your call, dropped everything, and spent their lives doing as you asked. I hear your call, too, and sense your knock at my heart's door. Please come in. Please make me sensitive to others you are drawing to you—people who need the good news of your love. Give me words to speak. Amen.

Week 2. Answering Three Important Questions

Scripture
- John 4:13-14; John 6:35-51 (Jesus Is Living Water and the Bread of Life)
- Matthew 16:18; 1 Corinthians 12:14-27; Acts 2:42-47 (The Work of the Church)
- Romans 12; Ephesians 4:1-6; 1 Thessalonians 5:11; Psalm 136 (What Your Church Offers)

Key Points
- Why do people need Jesus Christ? Jesus is the answer to our deepest needs.
- Why do people need the church? Jesus formed and called the church to carry out his mission.
- Why do people need *our* church? We have a unique witness in our community. What is it?

Response
I confess that I have been so concerned about the church meeting my own needs that I have prevented it from fully being the church Christ intends it to be in our community.

Prayer Focus
Dear God, we recognize that our church belongs to you. You desire to do more through us than we can ask or imagine. We confess, though, that there are times when we find ourselves in a spiritual rut personally and as a group. Help us rekindle our passion, and guide us to be the church you intend us to be, in the community and in the world. Amen.

Week 3. Making Visitors Feel Welcome

Scripture
- Romans 12:11-13 from *The Message* (Marks of a Christian)

Key Points
- Sometimes as churches we can burn out and just go through the motions.
- Dynamic, welcoming churches make sure that every opportunity for hospitality is effective.
- Hospitality is part of our mission in the world.

Response
I commit to finding ways to transform our church and its programs to welcome new people.

Prayer Focus
Dear God, help us practice welcome and hospitality. Show us the places where we need to change, and give us the courage an diligence to do what needs to be done. Give us hearts to welcome every person who walks through our doors. Guide us to be the church you intend us to be, in the community and in the world. Amen.

Week 4. Inviting Others to Grow in Faith

Scripture
- Romans 12:1-8 (New Life in Christ)
- 1 Corinthians 12, Ephesians 4:11-16 (Spiritual Gifts)

Key Points
- God planted gifts in each of us that are to be used to build up the community of faith.
- We are called to serve, not only to be served.
- Our gifts grow and unfold in new ways as we grow in faith and discipleship.

Response
I will discover my spiritual gifts and deploy them in our mission to reach people for Christ.

Prayer Focus
Dear God, thank you for the gifts you have planted in each of us. Help us to discover the ways that you call us to use these gifts, and give us the courage and diligence to use them. We pray that our church would be a place that meets a unique need in our community and that you would show us how to connect with people around us. Help us to be hospitable and welcoming, and use our gifts in ways that build up your church. Do a new thing in us, God. Amen.

PLANNING CALENDAR

Activity	Description	People	Dates

Phase 1. Examination

Activity	Description	People	Dates
Preparation	Invite leadership team	Pastor / leader	
	Order Program Guide with DVD-ROM	Pastor / leader	
	Distribute Program Guide to team • You may photocopy Program Guide • You may email Program Guide file (see DVD-ROM)	Pastor / leader	
Team meetings	Set schedule to read and discuss ideas presented in Program Guide Schedule should include: • Read and discuss "1. Becoming Relentlessly Outward Focused" • Read and discuss "2. Answering Three Important Questions" • Use "Check Point: Looking Inward" to debrief • Read and discuss "3. Attracting People in Your Community" • Read and discuss "4. Making Visitors Feel Welcome" • Read and discuss "5. Connecting and Following Up with Visitors" • Read and discuss "6. Inviting Others to Grow in Faith" • Use "Check Point: Moving Outward" to debrief	Leadership team	
Program planning	Organize teams and activities • Assign leadership of *Catch* teams • Schedule team meetings • Review and plan calendar of activities	Leadership team	

Phase 2. Teaching

Team meetings	Each *Catch* team meets regularly to discuss their plans and activities	*Catch* teams	
	Team leaders meet regularly for check-in and activity updates	Team leaders	

Small-group study	Plan and organize four-week small-group study
	• Set up *Catch* small groups and signup methods
	• Recruit leaders and schedule leader training
	• Determine method for tracking attendance
	• Invite congragation to small groups
	   o Bulletin announcements
	   o Church calendar
	   o Church newsletter
	   o Front page of church Web site
	• Announce start date of small groups
	• Order resources
	   o Small-Group Participant Book for each group member
	   o DVD with Leader Guide for each group
	• Coordinate with worship activities (see below)
		Connection team	

	Carry out four-week small-group study 1. Becoming Relentlessly Outward Focused 2. Answering Three Important Questions 3. Making Visitors Feel Welcome 4. Inviting Others to Grow in Faith	Small groups	
	After Session 4, sign up group members to get involved • Use "Ministry Descriptions and Commitment Form" (see DVD-ROM)		

Worship	Plan worship activities to take place during four-week teaching phase
	• Pastor plan sermons as needed
	• Worship team plan and coordinate other worship activities as needed
	   o Outreach moments
	   o Leadership team reports
	   o Highlight small-group study
		Worship team
		Pastor	

Phase 3. The Launch

Preparation	Reconvene leadership team to plan and stage the launch • Order Implementation Guide • Confirm steps for each team • Set followup meetings to coordinate team activities	Pastor Leadership team	
Marketing	Implement marketing campaign (see Implementation Guide for details) • Evaluate the current marketing effort and message • Plan your direct mail • Create information packets for visitors and materials for the connection center • Plan phone campaigns • Prepare newspaper and radio ads • Equip members to invite visitors	Marketing and Outreach Team	
Worship	Implement worship initiative (see Implementation Guide for details) • Create a Visitor-Friendly Worship Service	Worship Team	
Hospitality	Implement hospitality steps (see Implementation Guide for details) • Invite and train volunteer parking lot greeters • Invite and train a volunteer team of greeters • Encourage members to wear nametags • Create a visitor-friendly worship service • Establish a Connection Center • Establish or improve coffee time • Make room • Care for children • Evaluate phone greeting and voice mail information	Hospitality Team	
Connection	Follow up with visitors (see Implementation Guide for details) • Collect information about visitors • Follow up with first-time visitors • Follow up again after three visits • Be diligent in all connection and follow-up strategies •	Connection Team	
Membership	Facilitate path to membership (see Implementation Guide for details) • Invite returning visitors to join • Discipleship Pathway	Connection Team	

Small Group Participant Book Documents

MINISTRY DESCRIPTIONS AND COMMITMENT FORM

After participating in the *Catch* program, I am compelled to join a ministry team and get to work fishing for people. I understand that Jesus calls us to seek the least and the lost, and that means becoming an outward-focused church. I would like to join the following team:

_____Connection Point Ministry
Learning about church ministries and programs in order to connect visitors and members to them. Staffing the Connection Point desk and directing persons to their desired locations.

_____Mugging Ministry
Regularly delivering mugs / gifts as well as information about the church to first-time visitors. Volunteers will specify their delivery area and pick up mugs from a designated location each week.

_____Traffic Ministry
Perhaps working in conjunction with the trustees or building committee, this group will ensure adequate parking and assistance in the parking lot. In addition, this team will ensure that signage is clear and helpful from the minute a visitor pulls into the parking lot.

_____Marketing / Communications Ministry
This team will ensure that clear, thoughtful, well-designed communication pieces are sent out.

_____Welcoming Worship Ministry
Perhaps in conjunction with the greeters, ushers, and pastoral staff, this team will ensure that persons are greeted at the door, assisted to a seat, and given helpful information. In addition, this team will help make every person in the worship space feel welcomed and invited to participate.

_____Phone Ministry
This team will make cold calls using provided lists, inviting persons to worship as well as to various programs and events throughout the year.

_____Coffee with the Pastors Ministry
This team will work with the pastors to create a welcoming experience in which visitors are encouraged to become members. This may include providing refreshments, setting up or tearing down, and occasionally giving a testimony about being a member of your church.

Name _____

Address _____

Phone _____

Email _____

Implementation Guide Documents

1. Attracting People in Your Community

PHONE SCRIPT

Remember to smile! It comes across on the phone.

Show excitement and high energy!

Be a "caring caller." Listen for opportunities to connect and build relationships.

Make notes and fill in blanks.

Pray before you make each call.

Speak clearly.

> ➤ Hello, my name is _____ and I'm a volunteer with _____. How are you today / tonight? (Be prepared for someone *not* doing well. Be concerned and listen to their story, then offer consolation and pray for them if appropriate.)

No answer? Leave a message. See "Ring No Answer Script."

> ➤ We're making calls to let you know about something happening in our community. We want to invite you personally to our Easter / Christmas worship service.
> [or]
> We're preparing to launch a new church / ministry to serve our city. Do you already have a church home?
> ➤ [If yes] Then I want you to know what a joy it is to serve alongside you here in our city to reach people for Christ.
> ➤ [If no] Then I want you to know that I'm a part of an exciting church, and we're calling to invite people in the area to join us for _____. The event is at [time] at [location]. We're a church committed to meeting the needs of our community, and building fellowship and connection with one another. Our worship services are inspiring, and we offer great programs for people of all ages. If you've been looking for a church where you can ask questions about faith in a safe environment, where you can find meaningful opportunities to serve in the community, and where you can feel at home, we hope you will check us out.
> ➤ May I send you some information? [If yes, get the mailing address.] [If no:] Okay, thank you for your time. We're excited to be part of the community. You can also check us out at _____.org.
> ➤ Thank you for your time, and have a great day / night. God Bless!

RING NO ANSWER SCRIPT
(LEAVE MESSAGE)

Hello, my name is _____ and I'm a volunteer with _____. We're making calls to spread the word about our church. If you don't already have a church home, we'd like to invite you to check us out at _____.org, or you can call us at _____.

If you've been looking for a church where you can ask questions about faith in a safe environment, where you can find meaningful opportunities to serve the community, and where you can feel at home, we hope that you'll check us out. We're meeting at [time] at [location]. Thank you and God Bless!

SAMPLE RADIO AD

Here is a script from one of the radio ads that ran during the Christmas season:

The Gift on Behalf of Others

Are you looking for some last-minute gift ideas? Can't decide what to give someone who has everything?

Hi, I'm Adam Hamilton, senior pastor of the Church of the Resurrection. A friend recently gave me a great Christmas gift—a share of a sheep that was donated to a family in a third-world country. I recently gave a gift to a friend of ten meals provided in his honor to those who are homeless in a shelter here in Kansas City. If you're looking for a great gift to give someone who has everything, consider giving a gift in their honor to someone who has nothing. A gift of $10, $20, or $50 to area agencies that work with low-income people can make a difference and be a great way to let your friends and family know that you care about them and you care about others.

If you'd like help finding a way to give this kind of gift, check out our Web site at www.cor.org, where you can find links to area agencies and suggestions and opportunities for working directly with them to give gifts that really will make a difference. And if you don't yet have plans to attend a Christmas Eve candlelight service, I'd like to invite you to join us for one hour—an hour that will help you remember what Christmas is really all about.

2. Making Visitors Feel Welcome

WELCOMING LANGUAGE FOR WORSHIP

Greeting Script

Welcome to [church name]! We are so excited that you're here today! My name is [speaker's name]. I am [speaker's role or position], and we are so grateful that you've chosen to worship with us today!

Let's take a moment to welcome those sitting around you. Will you turn and say hello to a few people sitting around you?

We've gathered here to worship God, to sing praise to God's name, to lift up our prayers for thanksgiving and confession. We've come to lay before God our concerns. It's our hope that God will speak to you through the special music and the readings of Scripture and the message, that you might know God's will for your life. We hope you will leave renewed, refreshed, and ready to serve God in the world.

With that in mind, let's take a moment to pray.

Invitation to Fill Out Attendance Notebooks

The ushers are passing out the attendance notebooks. If you would take a few moments to let us know you were here, we would be most appreciative. If you're a first-time visitor, please notice the information provided for you. If you're a guest or a part of this congregation, please fill out the prayer cards to let us know how we can pray with and for you this week. As the notebooks get to the end of the row, please pass them back down the row, and look to see who is sitting near you so you can welcome those in your row by name at the end of our worship service.

As the notebook make their way down the rows, I want to take a minute to let you know what's going on in our community this week. [Make announcements.]

FIRST-TIME VISITOR TOUCH POINTS

Below are the "touch points" or contacts that a first-time visitor has available and may have received prior to, on the day of, and following their first visit to the church.

TOUCHES PRIOR TO WORSHIP SERVICE
- Web site, social media, or newspaper ad with worship times, phone number, and address.
- Contact with a receptionist during the week or Sunday mornings with voice mail backup that gives worship times, styles of worship, and directions to the church.
- Mailer received in home or given to a visitor by another member.
- Contact in the community through a service project or community outreach event, or by an outside group using the church building for an event.
- Volunteer prep teams prepare seatbacks, notebooks, bulletins, and coffee mugs during the week for weekend services.
- The worship team decorates the sanctuary and chapel beautifully for holidays.

TOUCHES ON THE DAY OF FIRST-TIME VISIT TO WORSHIP SERVICE
Before service
- Permanent signage is in place for first-time visitor parking, with instructions for visitors to turn on hazard lights as a signal to the parking attendants.
- Parking attendants on duty to direct traffic.
- Greeters located at all building entrances to give a warm welcome to visitors as they enter our church. Greeters wear a bright "greeter" button so they are easily identified.
- Guides will help visitors feel comfortable in our facilities by showing them the way to important locations, such as sanctuary, childcare, classrooms, and restrooms.
- Volunteers at the Connection Point (information center) are available to answer ministry questions or escort visitors to classes.
- Volunteers serve coffee before and after worship services.
- Ushers on duty at the sanctuary doors hand out bulletins and welcome everyone.
- Ushers on duty inside the sanctuary handle visitor seating, or ask for number in group and signal another usher to invite them to a seating area.

During service
- Acolytes carry in the cross and light the altar candles to remind us of Christ's presence with us.
- Service of worship planned with a first-time visitor in mind, engaging the congregation to encounter God through song, prayer, Scripture, and sermon.
- Time of greeting prior to the start of worship.
- Ushers pass attendance notebooks when directed to do so from the pulpit. (It is helpful that someone with authority asks everyone to sign in and that visitors see others signing in.)
- On days we serve communion, the communion team serves Holy Communion.

After service
- Ushers remove attendance sheets from notebooks and place them in two stacks—one for visitors and one for members.
- Volunteer teams record attendance in the database.

- First-time visitor attendance sheets are pulled from the visitor stack and given to the mapping team. These volunteers use the Internet to generate maps to first-time visitors' homes.
- Mappers place the maps in coffee mugs that are stuffed with a church brochure and other information. Mappers then place the mugs on shelves, according to zip code.
- Mug delivery team volunteers (a.k.a. "muggers") pick up the mugs and deliver them to first-time visitors' homes. Our goal is to deliver mugs within 48 hours of the first visit.
- First-time visitor information is entered into the database.

TOUCHES FOLLOWING FIRST-TIME VISIT

- First-time visitor letters are prepared on Monday evenings following completion of all data entry. The letter welcomes and thanks the visitor for worshiping with us. Letters are mailed on Tuesday.
- After visitor has attended three or more times within a three-month period, they receive a phone call, letter, or email with an invitation to Coffee with the Pastors.
- Weekday hospitality team volunteers are available at information booths to assist anyone with questions or directions to classrooms.
- Guided tours of the church are offered on weekends. Tours may also be scheduled by request.

3. Connecting and Following Up With Visitors

FIRST-TIME VISITOR LETTER

Dear _____,

Thank you for visiting [church name]. My hope is that you found the worship service uplifting and meaningful, and I want you to know that we would love to have you return again this coming weekend.

I also want you to know that we care about creating a great experience for our visitors. It is important to us and we welcome your feedback on how we did. Please take a moment to complete a very brief survey at [church Web site address]. As a small token of our appreciation, we have included with this letter a certificate for complimentary coffee. We hope you'll receive this with our thanks for helping us improve.

We've found that people connect into the life of our church quite easily. And making an early connection in service to others or through participation in a ministry of the church can make all the difference. If you or a friend or family member would like to hear about becoming more involved, please drop by the Connection Point at church or visit our Web site.

We hope that you will join us again for worship. And, if you are looking for a church home, we hope you'll get connected at [church name]. It would be an honor to be your church family.

Thank you again for your feedback. It is greatly appreciated.

Grace and Peace,

THIRD-TIME VISITOR LETTER

Dear _____,

We are so glad you are worshiping with us, and we pray that your experience has been a blessing. If you do not already have a church home, we hope you will consider being part of our congregation.

Though we are a growing church, most people find connecting into the life of our congregation easy. To explore ways to get connected, please stop by our Connection Point at church. We look forward to helping you connect with people who share your interests. Connecting with a "small group" makes it easier to feel at home here, and we offer a wide variety of small groups, classes, and activities to choose from. If you would like to learn more about the church on your own, please visit our Web site _____, which will answer questions you may have about our church.

If you think you might be interested in membership, I invite you to our next Coffee with the Pastors event on [date]. We will meet in [location]. Coffee with the Pastors provides additional information about the church and will help you discover how you can become connected. After the event, you can decide if you are ready to become a member of the church. To attend, simply let us know that you are coming by visiting [Web site address], or just call [person or office and phone number].

Again, we are very pleased that you joined us for worship! We would love to help you grow in your faith and share fellowship together. To speak with someone personally, please contact the church office at _____.

We have a passion for helping people connect into the life of the church!

In Christ,

4. Inviting Others to Grow in Faith

EMAIL INVITATION TO COFFEE WITH THE PASTORS

Attention, Visitors! Join Us for Coffee This Weekend

Are you a visitor to the church? If you are interested in finding out more about our church, or think you might be interested in membership, please join us for Coffee with the Pastors at [date, time, and location]. Childcare is provided.

You'll meet other visitors, find out about the church, and learn what is expected of you if you join. Then, at the end of the coffee, you'll have a chance to formally join the church if you are ready to do so.

Plan to attend Coffee with the Pastors, and then stay for the evening worship service. For more information, go to [Web site] or call [phone number].

FOLLOWUP LETTER TO COFFEE WITH THE PASTORS

Dear _____,

It was a great pleasure to welcome you at Coffee with the Pastors.

What are your next steps on the journey? You may want to consider becoming a member of the church. This commitment will make a world of difference, both in your life and in the lives of the people you will impact through ministry. Our church's staff and connection volunteers are always here to partner with you as you take your next step.

During the Coffee with the Pastors, you learned about our church's four membership expectations:
- Attend worship weekly, unless you are sick or out of town
- Grow in your faith beyond the weekly worship services
- Serve both within and beyond the walls of the church
- Give in proportion to your income, with the tithe being the goal

As we prepare for the upcoming year, we invite you to take the next step forward on your journey by participating in one of our learning communities, which were designed with you in mind. These are a great place to start.

[List learning opportunities and small groups]

May God bless you on your journey!

MEMBERSHIP FORM

Date _____

Worship Location: Central Campus ☐   Rez West ☐

FAMILY'S PRIMARY ADDRESS

_____
Address   City   State   Zip   Home Phone

HEAD(S) OF HOUSEHOLD JOINING TODAY

_____
Last Name   First   MI

_____
Preferred Name   Date of Birth: Mo/Day/Year

Gender: Male ☐   Female ☐

Marital Status: Single ☐   Couple ☐   Married ☐

_____
Cell Phone   Email

Baptized: Yes ☐ No ☐   Member of another church: Yes ☐ No ☐

_____
Church Name

_____
City   State   Zip

I WANT TO GET INVOLVED

I would like to know more about: (please check)

_____ Alpha   _____ Serving in Missions
_____ Learning Communities   _____ Serving at Resurrection
_____ Group Life   _____ Serving at FaithWork
_____ Children (thru 6th grade)   _____ Support Groups
_____ Students (7-12th grade)   _____ Congregational Care

Other _____

_____

CURRENT INVOLVEMENT (Please list all activities.)

Serving _____

_____

Growing in faith outside of worship _____

HEAD(S) OF HOUSEHOLD JOINING TODAY

_____
Last Name   First   MI

_____
Preferred Name   Date of Birth: Mo/Day/Year

Gender: Male ☐   Female ☐

Marital Status: Single ☐   Couple ☐   Married ☐

_____
Cell Phone   Email

Baptized: Yes ☐ No ☐   Member of another church: Yes ☐ No ☐

_____
Church Name

_____
City   State   Zip

I WANT TO GET INVOLVED

I would like to know more about: (please check)

_____ Alpha   _____ Serving in Missions
_____ Learning Communities   _____ Serving at Resurrection
_____ Group Life   _____ Serving at FaithWork
_____ Children (thru 6th grade)   _____ Support Groups
_____ Students (7-12th grade)   _____ Congregational Care

Other _____

_____

CURRENT INVOLVEMENT (Please list all activities.)

Serving _____

_____

Growing in faith outside of worship _____

CHILDREN JOINING

Last Name _____ First _____ MI ___
Preferred Name _____
Date of Birth: Mo/Day/Year _____ Gender: Male ☐ Female ☐
Baptized: Yes ☐ No ☐   Confirmed: Yes ☐ No ☐

Last Name _____ First _____ MI ___
Preferred Name _____
Date of Birth: Mo/Day/Year _____ Gender: Male ☐ Female ☐
Baptized: Yes ☐ No ☐   Confirmed: Yes ☐ No ☐

Last Name _____ First _____ MI ___
Preferred Name _____
Date of Birth: Mo/Day/Year _____ Gender: Male ☐ Female ☐
Baptized: Yes ☐ No ☐   Confirmed: Yes ☐ No ☐

Last Name _____ First _____ MI ___
Preferred Name _____
Date of Birth: Mo/Day/Year _____ Gender: Male ☐ Female ☐
Baptized: Yes ☐ No ☐   Confirmed: Yes ☐ No ☐

IMMEDIATE FAMILY MEMBERS **NOT JOINING** TODAY

Last Name _____ First _____ MI ___
Preferred Name _____
Date of Birth: Mo/Day/Year _____ Gender: Male ☐ Female ☐
Baptized: Yes ☐ No ☐   Confirmed: Yes ☐ No ☐

Last Name _____ First _____ MI ___
Preferred Name _____
Date of Birth: Mo/Day/Year _____ Gender: Male ☐ Female ☐
Baptized: Yes ☐ No ☐   Confirmed: Yes ☐ No ☐

HOW DID YOUR FAMILY LEARN ABOUT RESURRECTION? _____

_____

_____

LETTER TO NEW MEMBERS

Dear _____,

We are delighted to welcome you as a part of our church family. Our prayer is that your faith journey will be one filled with joy!

The purpose of this letter is to share with you some ways to progress toward becoming a "deeply committed Christian," which involves an intentional effort to grow in the areas of knowing, loving, and serving God outside of weekly worship.

For many, a worship service is the first step on this journey of faith. Maybe you've been attending here for two weeks, maybe ten years. Maybe you've already tried a few things; maybe you've just come each week and worshiped quietly. Regardless, there's a simple pathway for the journey of becoming a deeply committed Christian: begin with a learning community, and then commit to a small group. Though it's not the only path you can take, we know from experience that this one works well for many.

You have numerous resources at your immediate disposal. Your first stop is the Connection Point, where team members are on hand before and after worship to connect you with programming or service opportunities. Another option is taking an online mini self-assessment, which you will find at our church Web site.

At Coffee with the Pastors, we learned that membership expectations are:
- Attend worship weekly, unless you are sick or out of town
- Grow in your faith outside of worship, through Bible study and Christian community
- Serve both within and beyond the walls of the church
- Give in proportion to your income, with the tithe being the goal

If you requested information on your membership form about a ministry area, you will soon be contacted. In a few months we'll send you a short survey via email or U.S. mail. We would greatly appreciate your participation in the survey, as it helps us to know how we can improve our service to you.

Again, we are so pleased to have you in our church family!

Blessings to you!

NEW MEMBER SURVEY

Greetings to our newest members!

The purpose of this quick survey is to determine our effectiveness in helping you become a part of our church community. Our main desire is for our members to grow in their journey to know, love, and serve God.

We are committed to being an excellent resource to you as you get started. Thank you for your time!

Name
_____

1. I am currently attending worship
    - ○ Less than one time per month
    - ○ One time per month
    - ○ Two times per month
    - ○ Three times per month
    - ○ Four times per month

2. I am growing in faith outside worship
    - ○ Attending a learning community
    - ○ Through membership in a small group
    - ○ Not at this time
    - ○ Other (please specify)
    _____

3. I am serving / volunteering
    - ○ Not at this time
    - ○ This is how I'm serving
    _____

4. I understand that giving is an expression of my faith, with the tithe (10%) being the goal
    - ○ Yes
    - ○ No
    - ○ I want more information on this

5. How were you contacted after you joined the church?
    - ○ Phone
    - ○ Email
    - ○ I was not contacted

6. How do you rate the effectiveness of our current connection efforts?
    - Poor
    - Average
    - Good
    - Above average
    - Excellent

7. How could we improve our connection efforts?
   _____

8. I would like to be contacted about
   _____

9. The best way to contact me is by
    - Phone _____
    - Email _____

Thank you for completing this survey!

Appendix: Documents for Ministries and Planning

MINISTRY DESCRIPTIONS AND COMMITMENT FORM

After participating in the *Catch* program, I am compelled to join a ministry team and get to work fishing for people. I understand that Jesus calls us to seek the least and the lost, and that means becoming an outward-focused church. I would like to join the following team:

_____Connection Point Ministry
Learning about church ministries and programs in order to connect visitors and members to them. Staffing the Connection Point desk and directing persons to their desired locations.

_____Mugging Ministry
Regularly delivering mugs / gifts as well as information about the church to first-time visitors. Volunteers will specify their delivery area and pick up mugs from a designated location each week.

_____Traffic Ministry
Perhaps working in conjunction with the trustees or building committee, this group will ensure adequate parking and assistance in the parking lot. In addition, this team will ensure that signage is clear and helpful from the minute a visitor pulls into the parking lot.

_____Marketing / Communications Ministry
This team will ensure that clear, thoughtful, well-designed communication pieces are sent out.

_____Welcoming Worship Ministry
Perhaps in conjunction with the greeters, ushers, and pastoral staff, this team will ensure that persons are greeted at the door, assisted to a seat, and given helpful information. In addition, this team will help make every person in the worship space feel welcomed and invited to participate.

_____Phone Ministry
This team will make cold calls using provided lists, inviting persons to worship as well as to various programs and events throughout the year.

_____Coffee with the Pastors Ministry
This team will work with the pastors to create a welcoming experience in which visitors are encouraged to become members. This may include providing refreshments, setting up or tearing down, and occasionally giving a testimony about being a member of your church.

Name _____

Address _____

Phone _____

Email _____

MY MINISTRY COMMERCIAL

Once you are part of a church ministry, develop a thirty-second "commercial" about it. Your commercial should be a clear, concise, and compelling statement about the work your ministry area does; how that work makes a difference in people's lives; and why someone would want to consider volunteering their time and service to join your efforts. Be prepared to deliver this commercial at any time, so you can take advantage of unexpected, spur-of-the-moment opportunities to invite new people to volunteer with you.

STEP 1
Begin to create your commercial by answering the following questions relating to your ministry:

1. What does my ministry area do, ultimately?

2. How does it make a difference?

3. Why do I enjoy it?

4. What is the best part about the volunteer job I am recruiting for?

5. Why might others enjoy it?

STEP 2
Now, put your commercial together on the lines below using the ideas from your answers above. Add a strong closing question to inspire action. See the example below:

I volunteer for Habitat for Humanity. It's an exciting ministry because it allows me to meet new people and see a tangible difference when I serve. I've also enjoyed learning some new construction techniques. I know you enjoy working on home improvement projects. This would be a great place for you to volunteer. I'm volunteering next Saturday. Why don't you join me?

_____
_____
_____
_____
_____
_____

STEP 3
Practice your delivery. Remember to deliver your commercial with sincerity and enthusiasm. Let the joy you experience in serving shine through!

TRAFFIC MINISTRY

OBJECTIVES
- Serve the Lord
- Support the mission and ministry of the church
- Ensure a safe and positive worship experience
- Optimize the efficiency and safety of traffic flow
- Minimize automobile and pedestrian cross-traffic
- Greet worshipers, volunteers, and staff as they enter and leave facility
- Assist in emergency situations
- Have fun and enjoy the fellowship

HELPFUL TIPS

Wear weather-appropriate clothing.
    Summer – Loose fitting, light materials, sun protection, hat
    Winter – Layers for warmth, including thermal socks, thermal gloves, thermal headwear, thermal face and ear protection
    Spring / fall – Layers that allow you flexibility depending on the changing weather conditions

Wear brightly colored clothing.
    Traffic safety vests and traffic ministry hats will be provided, but the more visible the better.

Wear comfortable, supportive footwear.
    You will be on your feet for an extended duration, so make sure your feet are comfortable.
    If the weather is wet or snowy, ensure that your footwear is waterproof.

When the weather is sunny, wear sunglasses.
    It can get bright out there!

When the weather is rainy, wear a rain suit or poncho.
    Rain ponchos are provided. If you have a rain suit, it will keep you much drier.

When it is dark, wear reflective gear.
    Always carry a flashlight or LED traffic wand.

When you are in close proximity to traffic, be sensitive to your surroundings.
    When you direct cars to stop, make sure they do so before you direct others.

When working pedestrian crossings, manage individuals walking just as you would vehicle traffic.
    Hold the cars for people to walk, and hold the people for cars to pass.
    In inclement weather, give pedestrians priority over vehicles.

When you encounter problems, immediately notify your team leader.
    Problems can range from health issues to situational issues.

Take advantage of breaks.
> Get off your feet, use the restroom, have a snack, warm up or cool down.
> Drink fluids. Hydration is important in both warm and cold weather.

When individuals don't take direction, be courteous.
> Let them go unless it increases the risk for pedestrians or other motorists.

ADDITIONAL COMMENTS

For the most part, everyone will be friendly and appreciative of your efforts. Periodically, however, you will encounter individuals who are angry or upset. The best way to respond is simply to smile and tell them you are a volunteer and are doing your best. If the problem persists, immediately contact your team leader.

If you do not understand the responsibilities of the position you have been assigned, please ask your team leader for clarification before taking the position. If you are not comfortable with the task assigned, please request a change from your team leader.

Have a great time, and remember that the traffic team provides the first impression for visitors when they arrive and the last impression when they leave.

Have fun, and enjoy the fellowship!

GREETER MINISTRY

PURPOSE STATEMENT
To reflect the love of Christ by being welcoming, hospitable, and gracious to those who enter our church home.

MINISTRY SCRIPTURE VERSE
"As God's chosen one, holy and beloved, clothes yourselves with compassion, kindness, humility, meekness and patience" (Colossians 3:12).

GREETER MINISTRY OBJECTIVES

Be faithful to your commitment
Consistency in attendance is vital to this ministry. We can never have too many greeters!

Take ownership
Set the tone. Be relaxed and cheerful in welcoming everyone, including children.

Stay at your assigned door
Direct anyone having questions or needing assistance to the Connection Point, or to one of the worship welcome guides. When giving people directions, never point the way. Always escort them, while being mindful not to leave the door(s) attended.

Display enthusiasm
Your excitement about your church home will make a difference to others.

Generate an atmosphere of care
Warmly receive and welcome everyone. Watch for those who need a hand opening doors or managing babies or young children, especially in inclement weather.

GREETER TEAM TIPS
- Pray before you begin your shift. Be thankful for the blessings of the day, and ask God to shine through you as you represent the church. "And we, who with unveiled faces all reflect the Lord's glory, are being transformed into his likeness with ever-increasing glory, which comes from the Lord, who is the Spirit" (2 Corinthians 3:18).
- Arrive at least thirty minutes prior to the service, and stay until most of the latecomers have arrived.
- Wear your nametag, and collect your greeter badge from the head greeter at the Connection Point before proceeding to your assigned position.
- Please find a substitute if you are not able to keep your scheduled commitment. Keep the roster of your team handy so you can call or email someone to switch weeks with you or take your place.
- If your friends want to stop and talk, please tell them you are "on duty" and you will be happy to catch up with them later.
- Be flexible. Changes will arise, and when they do, remember that you are serving the Lord.

CONNECTION POINT MINISTRY

DESCRIPTION
This team conducts all activities before, during, and after worship services at the Connection Point, the church's information center.

TEAM ACTIVITIES INCLUDE
Consultants are stationed at the Connection Point at each worship service to help integrate members and visitors into the life of our church. Consultants will offer the "20,000-foot view" of all ministries and ministry paths into the church.

Referrals - Consultants will log referrals for subsequent follow-up. These referrals will be related to the ministry area on the Monday following the weekend, using the church database referral system.

Tools - Consultants utilize the following information tools while serving at the Connection Point:
1. Weekly update binder for current team communications and processes
2. Shift notes (located in weekly update binder)
3. Connection Point ministry information binder
4. Ministry index
5. Church Web site
6. Ministry literature
7. Weekly calendar
8. Current volunteer listing
9. Spiritual self-assessment
10. Weekly emails from team leadership with important information on current opportunities
11. Grace for yourself and others! You cannot know everything – no one can. All we can do is our best.

Consultants stay abreast of current connection opportunities within the church and access the computer and / or ministry brochures as needed.

Spiritual mini-assessment - During one-on-one discussion, the consultant may utilize the spiritual self-assessment to help map out ministry options for individuals who visit the Connection Point.

Hospitality duties - Consultants will also perform hospitality duties when needed including: nametag preparation, will-call retrieval, and emergency procedures.

Emergencies - Consultants will be familiar with emergency processes in the event of an emergency situation.

SCHEDULE
Consultants will staff the Connection Point for a minimum of one shift per month before and after worship. Consultants should arrive a half hour before worship and not leave until most worshipers have arrived and worship has begun. Consultants should leave worship shortly before the service is over in order to be at the Connection Point as worshipers exit.

Substitutes - If unable to serve at a shift due to illness, travel, or a personal issue, consultants will find a substitute by personally contacting (a) shiftmates and (b) all teammates, alerting the shift leader about who will be substituting. Consultants will make every effort to find a substitute in advance. Often, shiftmates will trade shifts if contacted in advance. (Note: A phone call to a teammate is often more effective than a "wallpaper" email to all shiftmates.)

Annual / Shift Meetings - Approximately three shift meetings and/or all-team meetings in addition to a Christmas celebration are held each year. Consultants will attend at least one meeting each year (in addition to the Christmas celebration) to get to know their teammates and stay abreast of processes, ministry needs, activities, and other issues.

SPIRITUAL GIFTS AND PERSONALITY STYLES
Extrovert / stable; extrovert / flexible

Spiritual gifts that are typically found in someone serving in this role:
- Administration
- Discernment of spirits
- Exhortation
- Assistance/helps

Passions and skills that are typically found in someone serving in this role:
- Counseling
- Administration skills
- Encouragement of others
- Communication
- Helping / counseling
- Good listening skills
- Hospitality
- Organization
- Spiritual growth
- Christian Community

MUGGING MINISTRY

PURPOSE STATEMENT
To reflect the love of Christ by being welcoming, hospitable, and gracious to those who enter our church home.

MINISTRY SCRIPTURE VERSE
"As God's chosen one, holy and beloved, clothes yourselves with compassion, kindness, humility, meekness and patience" (Colossians 3:12).

MUG DELIVERY TEAM TIPS
When delivering mugs, remember that you are a special representative of the church. Most importantly, you are a representative of Christ!

- Try to deliver the mugs within seventy-two hours after a person's first visit. Mugs can be found at the mug station in the narthex, sorted by zip code.
- A map will be enclosed with each mug to be delivered. If delivering more than one mug, plan your journey ahead of time to take the most direct and efficient route.
- Ring the visitor's doorbell. If the visitor answers, introduce yourself. For example: "My name is_____. I am from _____ and I don't want to come in. I just want to thank you for visiting our church and to give you, as a token of our appreciation, a small gift. (Hand them the mug or gift.) I am glad to answer any questions for you. Again, we just wanted to let you know how much we loved having you in worship, and if you don't have a church home, we wanted you to know it would be an honor for us to be your church family. I hope to see you again soon in worship."
- If they have questions, answer to the best of your knowledge. If you are not sure about something, tell them you will have someone contact them with the answer. After leaving, write a note with the visitor's question, attach it to the map, and return it to the the mug station in the narthex.
- If no one answers the door, jot a quick note to leave with the mug. For example: "Sorry to have missed you. Hope you worship with us again soon! Blessings, (and your name)." Leave the mug on the front porch or in an area where it will be seen when the visitor returns home. If there is a phone number on the map, give the visitor a call to indicate you are sorry you missed them and that you left a mug by the door.
- If delivering to a gated apartment complex, go to the office to see if they will let you in the gate. (If you have the apartment number, most will let you in. If you don't, ask the office personnel if they will please make sure the visitor receives the mug.) Again, if you have a phone number, you can call the visitor to let them know you left a mug at the office.
- The next time you are at church, return the maps to the drop box at the mug station in the narthex. Please note that the names, addresses, and phone numbers provided are to be used for church purposes only. Any violation will be considered an abuse of trust.

Thank you for volunteering your time and making a difference by reaching out through this ministry. "I do it all for the sake of the gospel, that I may share in its blessings" (1 Corinthians 9:23).

DVD ROM Contents

VIDEOS

1. Becoming Relentlessly Outward Focused (3:05)

2. Answering Three Important Questions

- Why Do People Need Jesus Christ? (1:51)
- Why Do People Need the Church? (1:34)
- Why Do People Need *Your* Church? (3:12)

3. Attracting People in Your Community

- Church Communications (3:50)
- Strategic Marketing (3:20)
- Direct Mail Marketing (4:58)
- Christmas Eve Worship Promotion (3:34)
- Careful Creative Execution (3:04)
- Newspaper Advertising (2:23)
- Dynamic Website (1:46)

4. Making Visitors Feel Welcome

- Making Visitors Feel Welcome (3:53)
- A Welcoming Worship Environment (2:57)
- Welcoming and Greeting Newcomers (1:59)
- A Welcoming Worship Experience (3:50)
- Extending a Welcome During the Service (2:29)
- Getting to Know Your Church Visitor (4:04)
- Faithful to Jesus' Command (1:59)

5. Connecting and Following Up with Visitors (6:55)

6. Inviting Others to Grow in Faith (10:22)

DOCUMENTS

Program Guide Documents
- Check Point: Looking Inward (see p. 39)
- Check Point: Moving Outward (see p. 95)
- Inviting the Leadership Team
- Sermon Helps and Key Scriptures
- Planning Calendar
- Program Guide—For Duplication (see DVD ROM)

Small Group Participant Book Documents
- Ministry Descriptions and Commitment Form

Implementation Guide Documents

1. Attracting People in Your Community
- Phone Script
- Ring No Answer Script
- Sample Radio Ad

2. Making Visitors Feel Welcome
- Welcoming Language for Worship
- First-Time Visitor Touch Points

3. Connecting and Following Up With Visitors
- First-Time Visitor Letter
- Third-Time Visitor Letter

4. Inviting Others to Grow in Faith
- Email Invitation to Coffee with the Pastors
- Follow-Up Letter to Coffee with the Pastors
- Sample Membership Form
- Letter to New Members
- New Member Survey

Appendix: Documents for Ministries and Planning

- Ministry Descriptions and Commitment Form
- My Ministry Commercial
- Traffic Ministry
- Greeter Ministry
- Connection Point Ministry
- Mugging Ministry
- Planning Calendar